# The book on flipping houses

## A Beginner's Guide to Profitable Real Estate Investment

**By Christopher P. Witson**

The Book on Flipping Houses/Christopher P.Witson

## copyright

© [2024] by Christopher P. Witson. All rights reserved.

## Disclaimer

This book is intended only for educational and instructional reasons, and any information included inside it remains confidential. While every attempt has been made to guarantee its correctness, the author and publisher make no representations or warranties about the accuracy or completeness of the contents of this book. The author and publisher shall not be responsible for any loss of profit or any other commercial damages, including but not limited to special, incidental, consequential, or other damages. It is strongly recommended that readers carry out their independent research and seek the advice of specialists before making any choices on investments or engaging in any real estate transactions. The

The author and publisher disclaim all liability for the use or interpretation of the material included in this book.

# About the author

Christopher P. Witson is a seasoned real estate expert.

entrepreneur and thought leader in the dynamic field of the real estate industry. With a wealth of knowledge and skills spanning over two decades, Christopher has established himself as a valued counsellor, mentor, and champion for prospective investors and homeowners alike.

As a Realtor, Christopher has helped many customers manage the difficulties of purchasing, selling, and investing in real estate assets. His devotion to offering great service, individualized assistance, and unsurpassed experience has earned him a remarkable reputation among customers and colleagues alike.

Beyond his position as a real estate specialist, Christopher is a passionate entrepreneur with a good eye for recognizing attractive investment possibilities and generating new solutions to suit market needs. His entrepreneurial energy and forward-thinking attitude have propelled the success of countless businesses in the real estate market.

Christopher is devoted to sharing his expertise, thoughts, and techniques with those who strive to prosper in the competitive field of the real estate industry. Through his publications, speaking engagements, and mentoring programs, he enables people to realize their real estate objectives, generate wealth, and establish sustainable financial independence.

Whether you are a first-time homeowner, seasoned investor, or aspiring entrepreneur, Christopher P. Witson's experience and assistance are vital tools on your route to success in the ever-evolving arena of real estate. Connect with Christopher now and open the doors to your future in real estate expertise.

# Table Of Contents

**Introduction**     **11**
    Understanding house flipping:Investors benefits and opportunities     12
    Overview of the development of house flipping     17
    Exciting Opportunities in Real Estate     19

**Getting Started: Investing in Real Estate**     **25**
    Networking and Building Relationships     42
    Dynamics to enhance your chance of success in the competitive real estate market     52
    Understanding the Basics of Real Estate Investment     56
    Building a Strong Financial Foundation for Real Estate Investing     59
    Setting Realistic Goals for House Flipping     62
    Creating a Timeline     69
    Importance of Having a Timeline     69
    Master Timeline for Multiple House Flips     71
    Key Considerations for Multiple Flips     74
    Leverage the Power of Outsourcing to Supercharge Your House Flips     75

**Building a Reliable Team**     **81**
    Importance of Having a Reliable Team     81
    Characteristics of an Ideal Team     82
    Building a Reliable Team     83

| | |
|---|---|
| Prioritizing and Organizing Tasks | 85 |
| Managing Finances | 88 |
| How to handle expenses for several home flips | 89 |
| Helpful tools and software for managing money | 91 |
| Communication | 92 |

**Protecting Yourself: Liability Insurance** — **95**

| | |
|---|---|
| Is insurance required when flipping houses? | 96 |
| How Much Protection Do You Need From Insurance? | 99 |
| What is the cost of insurance on a flip? | 102 |
| When should you get insurance for your flip? | 103 |
| Importance of Liability Insurance for House Flippers | 105 |
| How to Find Affordable Insurance Option | 108 |
| Exploring Different Strategies And Sources for Finding Properties | 126 |
| 5 Best Cities To Flip Houses 2024 | 135 |
| Identifying potential investment opportunities | 140 |
| Why Networking Matters for Real Estate Professionals | 145 |
| Where to Find Networking Opportunities | 147 |
| Strategies to Enhance Your Networking Game | 149 |

**Doing Your Homework: Due Diligence** — **153**

| | |
|---|---|
| Conducting thorough property research | 157 |
| Understanding Neighborhood and Market Trends | 168 |
| Evaluating potential risks and challenges | 174 |

**Renovating for Profit: Adding Value to the Property**

**181**
    Essential Renovations and Improvements    185
    Budgeting and Managing Renovation Costs    192
        Importance Of Budgeting And Managing Renovation Costs    193
    Hands-On or Help Wanted? Deciding What to Tackle Yourself During Your Remodel    202
    Level Up Your Flip: How to Recruit the Best Contractors for Every Job    208

**Selling the Deal: Marketingand Negotiation Strategies**    **211**
    Mastering the Art of Negotiation: Communication Strategies for Success    216
    Crafting a Winning Offer: Make a Strong First Impression    217
    What should your marketing convey?    229
    Sale By Owner Vs. Realtor    231
    Pricing Strategies for Maximum Profit    246

**Valuing Your Investment: Methods of Valuation**    **267**
    Understanding Different Valuation Methods    268
        Comparable Methods    268
        The Income Approach Method    286
        Cost Approach Method:    302
    Appraisal Techniques for Flipped Properties    316
    Factors Influencing Property Valuation    329

**Managing Financial Aspects: Mortgage Loans and Total Cost of Ownership**    **345**
    Exploring Mortgage Options for Financing Flips    350

Calculating Total Cost of Ownership 356
    The relevance of the total cost of ownership 357
    Managing Cash Flow and Expenses Effectively 360

**Navigating Market Dynamics: AvoidingManipulation 365**
    Recognizing Market Manipulation Tactics 369

**Conclusion: Your Journey to Success in House Flipping 389**
    Recap of Key Concepts and Strategies 390
    Encouragement to Take Action and Pursue Your Real Estate Goals 393
    Resources for Further Learning and Support 395

# Introduction

Have you ever fantasized about uncovering a hidden gem beneath layers of neglect? Maybe a charming colonial peeking through overgrown vines or a mid-century modern masterpiece waiting to be reborn from crumbling plaster. House flipping promises the thrill of transforming forgotten houses into financial windfalls. But let's face it, reality TV doesn't always show the full picture.

This book isn't interested in perpetuating flipping myths. We'll crack open the secrets professional house flippers use, but with a crucial difference: we'll equip you to avoid the "flop" and turn those hidden gems into glittering profits.

Here's what you'll discover:

***Beyond the Dream Flip:*** We strip away the glamor to reveal the realities of house flipping, from uncovering hidden problems to outsmarting budget-busting surprises.

***From Dust Bowl to Dream Home:*** Learn how to identify properties brimming with potential and transform them into homes buyers can't resist.

***The Flip Whisperer's Toolkit:*** Build your dream team of contractors, lenders, and renovation ninjas with our proven strategies.

This book is your chance to flip the script on house flipping. Are you ready to unlock the secrets to financial freedom and transform fixer-upper dreams into reality? Ditch the demolition drama and grab your copy today.

## Understanding house flipping: Investors benefits and opportunities

House flipping is a real estate investment technique where an investor acquires a house with the purpose of remodeling or upgrading it and then sells it for a profit. The procedure often entails purchasing a property that is undervalued or in need of repairs, performing smart renovations or enhancements to boost its market worth, and then selling it at a higher price.

The purpose of home flipping is to create a profit by selling the property soon once improvements are done. Successful home flippers frequently have a deep awareness of the local real estate market, the expenditures involved with repairs, and the prospective resale value of the property.

House flipping may be a rewarding financial strategy, but it also comes with hazards. Flippers must carefully manage their funds, precisely estimate remodeling expenditures, and accurately analyze market circumstances to achieve a successful flip. Additionally, unanticipated delays or issues during the refurbishment process might cut into potential revenues.

Flipping homes entails acquiring a property, especially one that needs repairs or improvements, with the purpose of immediately reselling it for a profit. Here is a more extensive review of home flipping and its benefits:

***Purchase of Undervalued Homes:*** House flippers generally target homes that are undervalued or distressed, meaning they may be acquired at a cheaper price than their prospective market worth. This gives investors a chance to profit from the gap between the purchase price and the property's real value.

***Renovation and Improvement:*** After purchasing a home, house flippers invest in renovations and upgrades to boost its attractiveness and raise its market value. This could involve cosmetic changes like painting and landscaping, as well as more serious renovations such as kitchen or bathroom remodels. By investing in targeted modifications, flippers try to entice buyers prepared to pay a premium for a move-in ready or upgraded house.

***Quick Turnaround:*** The potential for a quick turnaround is one of the main advantages of house flipping. Unlike buy-and-hold real estate investments, where investors gain revenue via rental income over time, home flipping enables investors to achieve profits very rapidly. In order to minimize holding costs and maximize profits, flippers work quickly to complete renovations and sell the property.

***Potential for High Returns:*** Successful property flips may offer considerable gains for investors. Flippers may make significant returns on their investment if they buy properties for less than market value, renovate them to increase their value, and then sell them for a higher price. While the precise profit margin varies based on variables such as the property's location, condition, and market circumstances, expert flippers may obtain double-digit returns on their investment.

***Flexibility and Control:*** House flipping allows investors a great degree of flexibility and control over their investing plan. Flippers have the opportunity to pick which houses to acquire, how much to spend on improvements, and when to sell. This degree of control enables investors to adjust their strategy to meet their financial objectives, risk tolerance, and market circumstances.

***Diversification:*** House flipping may serve as a vital component of a diversified financial portfolio. By integrating real estate investments with stocks, bonds, and other assets, investors may diversify risk and perhaps boost total profits. Additionally, real estate frequently demonstrates a minimal correlation with conventional financial markets, offering diversification advantages and helping to alleviate portfolio volatility. The development of home flipping spans decades, with its origins dating back to prehistoric times.

# Overview of the development of house flipping

How can something become more generally known? Typically, when something shows up on television in some way, everyone sees it, learns about it, or is somewhat acquainted with it. Such is the scenario with "flipping houses." Three decades ago, most people would not have realized what a home flipper was. However, the term is now more well-known due to several TV programs and other media. There have always been home flippers, even during the colonial period and in pre-colonial England before the United States was colonized. House flipping was originally confined to a small number of people in a community who had the time, finances, and willingness to do it. However, these days, anybody can afford to do it, even those who are not considered "wealthy."

There was a recession in the economy in the 1980s. Earnings in the stock market declined, but home foreclosures soared. As the market improved, clever people would acquire foreclosures, fix them, and then flip them for a profit. Thus, the late 1980s witnessed the actual birth of American home flipping in the contemporary sense.

In the 1980s and 1990s, as new housing was developed at an increasing pace, refurbishing existing houses also gained appeal. Media figures like Bob Vila and television series like "This Old House" pushed average people to restore instead of destroying their houses. Giants such as Lowe's and Home Depot erected their large shops in practically every American suburban area, enabling the process of "doing it yourself" home improvement projects for the ordinary Joe and Jane.

Nowadays, people who have considered remodeling older homes are not limited to carpenters or contractors. The typical individual may find a lot of information online these days to aid them in completing undertakings; merely take a look at all the "How To" YouTube videos that are available.

While most individuals repair their own homes so they can remain in them, an increasing number of relatively young businesses in their 20s and 30s are converting residences into successful companies. They acquire an inexpensive property and either live there alone or with professional aid while they make repairs. Then, after a few months, they invest in it and "flip" it for a profit, making more money than they initially spent on it. After that, the flippers walk on to the next home and do it again. Nowadays, it looks to be a profitable vocation if and when rivalry is avoided.

## Exciting Opportunities in Real Estate

Exciting prospects exist in the area of real estate, giving investors a varied assortment of routes to investigate. Here is why real estate provides such promise:

***Diverse Investment Options:*** Real estate offers a broad variety of investment options, from residential properties like single-family homes and condos to commercial assets such as office buildings, retail spaces, and industrial warehouses. Additionally, investors might investigate alternative real estate assets, including holiday rentals, real estate investment trusts (REITs), and crowdfunding platforms. This variety enables investors to adjust their investing plan to their tastes, risk tolerance, and financial objectives.

***Consistent income creation:*** Real estate investments provide the possibility for consistent income creation via rental revenue. The rental payments made by tenants to rental properties provide investors with a consistent stream of income, frequently on a monthly basis. This money may be utilized to fund operational expenditures, including mortgage payments, and provide passive income for investors. Additionally, rental income has the potential to expand over time as rentals rise and property values improve.

***Increase potential:*** Real estate has traditionally shown the potential for long-term increase in value. Properties tend to increase over time owing to reasons such as inflation, population expansion, and rising demand for housing. As property prices grow, investors may achieve capital gains by selling their homes at a higher price than what they purchased. This appreciation may add to the total development of an investor's real estate portfolio and act as a source of wealth creation.

***Tax benefits:*** Real estate investments provide different tax benefits that may help investors decrease their tax obligations and enhance their earnings. Investors may deduct expenditures such as property taxes, mortgage interest, insurance premiums, and depreciation from their taxable income. Additionally, real estate investments may qualify for preferential tax treatment, such as capital gains tax rates for properties held for more than one year and the option to delay taxes via like-kind swaps.

***Portfolio Diversification:*** Real estate offers the potential for portfolio diversification, enabling investors to disperse risk across multiple asset classes and investment types. Real estate generally demonstrates poor correlation with conventional financial assets like stocks and bonds, meaning its performance may not move in sync with the larger market. By integrating real estate into a diversified investment portfolio, investors may minimize overall portfolio volatility and boost risk-adjusted returns.

***Concrete Asset Ownership:*** Real estate investments give the concrete advantage of owning real assets with inherent worth. Unlike stocks or bonds, which reflect ownership in businesses or financial obligations, real estate gives investors physical assets that they can see, touch, and manage. This physical feature of real estate ownership may offer investors a feeling of security and stability, as well as the possibility for personal pleasure via property usage or rental revenue.

# Getting Started: Investing in Real Estate

***Identify your objectives:*** Determining your investing goals implies declaring your hopes and desires for your real estate operations. This is a critical step, as it offers direction for your investing plan and helps you stay focused on your objectives.

**Budgetary Objectives:** Think about the financial objectives you have for your real estate investment. Is your objective to develop passive income to supplement your existing income? Do you want to create long-term wealth and guarantee your retirement?

***Risk Tolerance:*** Assess your comfort level with risk. Real estate investment comes with variable degrees of risk based on factors including property type, location, and market circumstances. Some investments may provide larger potential returns but come with increased risk, while others may provide more stability but lower profits. Understanding your risk tolerance can help you pick assets that fit with your comfort level.

***Investment timeframe:*** Determine your investment timeframe or horizon. Are you seeking short-term chances to earn rapid gains, such as flipping homes, or are you interested in long-term investments like rental properties? Your investment timeframe will impact your approach and the types of properties you choose.

own tastes Consider your own tastes and lifestyle objectives. Do you appreciate hands-on engagement in property management, or do you prefer a more passive investing approach? Are you interested in investing locally, where you can manage properties directly, or are you open to investigating possibilities in other markets? Your own tastes will impact your investing approach and the types of properties you seek.

***Overall Objective:*** Think about the bigger picture and what you eventually intend to accomplish through real estate investment. Are you hoping to attain financial independence, build a legacy for your family, or follow a special passion or interest? Understanding your broad objectives can help you stay motivated and focused on your long-term goals. By defining your investing objectives, you may personalize your real estate investment plan to correspond with your financial goals, risk tolerance, and personal preferences. This clarity will guide your decision-making process and boost your chances of success in real estate investment.

***Educate oneself:*** Educating oneself about the foundations of real estate investment is vital for success in the sector.

## Why education?

***Understanding ideas:*** Real estate investment incorporates many ideas and principles that you need to master to make educated selections. These include property assessment (determining the worth of a property), financing alternatives (methods for funding your assets), and market analysis (assessing market developments and circumstances). Without a firm knowledge of these foundations, you may struggle to manage the complexity of real estate investment.

***Making informed choices:*** Education helps you make informed choices regarding your real estate investments. By knowing topics like property valuation, you may effectively estimate the worth of possible investment properties and decide if they correspond with your investing objectives. Similarly, understanding financing choices helps you investigate numerous methods to finance your investments and pick the most suitable financing plan for your requirements.

***Minimizing hazards:*** Real estate investment naturally contains hazards, but knowledge may help you limit these risks. By learning about market analysis, you can identify emerging trends and potential pitfalls in the market, allowing you to make proactive decisions to mitigate risks. Additionally, knowing property value helps you avoid overpaying for properties and decreases the danger of financial losses.

***Maximizing profits:*** Education empowers you with the skills and methods to optimize profits on your real estate investments. By understanding financing possibilities, you may use multiple financing techniques to boost your spending power and maximize your investment returns. Similarly, knowledge of market analysis allows you to identify opportunities for value appreciation and capitalize on emerging market trends.

***Continuous Learning:*** Real estate investing is a dynamic and evolving field, so ongoing education is essential for success. By staying informed about changes in market conditions, regulations, and investment strategies, you can adapt your approach to remain competitive and capitalize on new opportunities. Whether through books, seminars, online courses, or networking with industry professionals, continuous learning is key to staying ahead in real estate investing.

***Assess Your finances:*** Assessing your finances is a critical step in real estate investing as it helps you understand your financial capabilities and make informed decisions. Here's how you can go about evaluating your financial situation:

***Review your savings:*** Take stock of your savings, including cash reserves and other liquid assets. Determine how much money you have available to invest in real estate without jeopardizing your emergency fund or other financial obligations.

***Evaluate Your Income:*** Assess your regular income sources, including wages, salaries, rental income, or business profits. Consider how much disposable income you have available after covering essential expenses like housing, utilities, and groceries.

***Check Your Credit Score:*** Obtain a copy of your credit report and check your credit score. A good credit score is essential for securing favorable financing terms and interest rates when purchasing investment properties. If your credit score is lower than desired, take steps to improve it before applying for loans or mortgages.

***Consider Existing Debt:*** Evaluate your existing debt obligations, including credit card balances, student loans, auto loans, and mortgages. Determine your debt-to-income ratio, which compares your monthly debt payments to your gross monthly income. Lenders use this ratio to assess your ability to manage additional debt and may require a certain debt-to-income ratio to qualify for loans.

***Calculate Your Investment Capacity:*** Based on your savings, income, credit score, and existing debt, calculate how much you can afford to invest in real estate. Consider factors like down payments, closing costs, renovation expenses, and ongoing maintenance costs when estimating your investment capacity.

***Set a budget:*** Establish a realistic budget for your real estate investments based on your financial assessment. Determine how much you're willing to invest in individual properties and allocate funds for potential expenses like property taxes, insurance, repairs, and vacancies.

***Seek professional advice:***Consider consulting with a financial advisor or mortgage broker to get personalized guidance on your real estate investment options. A financial professional can help you assess your financial situation, explore financing options, and develop a comprehensive investment plan tailored to your goals and risk tolerance.

***Examine Your Financing Options:*** Real estate investments often require substantial capital, so you may need to explore financing options such as mortgages, loans, or partnerships. Research different lenders and loan programs to find the best fit for your needs. Financing is a crucial aspect of real estate investing, especially considering the substantial capital often required.

## Exploring my financial options

***Mortgages:*** Many real estate investors utilize mortgages as a springboard to launch their investment journey. With a mortgage, you borrow money from a lender to purchase a property, and the property serves as collateral for the loan. Mortgages typically require a down payment, which is a percentage of the property's purchase price. The lender then provides the remaining funds, and you repay the loan over time with interest. Different types of mortgages are available, including conventional mortgages, FHA loans, VA loans, and USDA loans, each with its own eligibility requirements and terms.

*Loans:* In addition to traditional mortgages, there are various types of loans available for real estate investors. For example, you may consider a home equity loan or home equity line of credit (HELOC), which allow you to borrow against the equity in your existing property to finance a new investment. Alternatively, you could explore personal loans, private loans, or hard money loans, which are often used for short-term financing or when traditional financing is not available.

***Partnerships:*** Another option is to form partnerships with other investors or lenders to pool resources and share the financial burden of real estate investments. Partnerships can take various forms, such as joint ventures, limited partnerships, or syndications, depending on the level of involvement and risk-sharing arrangements. Partnering with individuals or entities with complementary skills, expertise, or financial resources can provide access to additional capital and expand your investment opportunities.

***Research and Comparison:*** When exploring financing options, it's essential to research different lenders and loan programs to find the best fit for your needs. Compare interest rates, loan terms, fees, and eligibility requirements from multiple lenders to ensure you're getting the most favorable terms possible. Consider factors like your credit score, income, debt-to-income ratio, and investment objectives when selecting a financing option.

***Start Small:*** Consider starting with a smaller investment, such as purchasing a single-family home or a condominium, before taking on larger projects. Starting small allows you to gain experience, build confidence, and minimize risk as you learn the ropes of real estate investing. Starting small in real estate investing is a prudent approach that offers several advantages.

Why beginning with a smaller investment, such as purchasing a single-family home or a condominium, can be beneficial:

***Lower financial risk:*** Smaller investments typically require less capital upfront compared to larger projects like commercial properties or multifamily units. By starting small, you can minimize financial risk and exposure while gaining valuable experience in real estate investing.

***Easier Financing:*** Smaller properties are often more accessible in terms of financing. Lenders may be more willing to extend financing for single-family homes or condominiums, especially if you have limited experience or resources. This makes it easier to secure funding and get started with your first investment property.

***Manageable Maintenance:*** Single-family homes and condominiums generally have lower maintenance costs and fewer management responsibilities compared to larger properties. With a smaller investment, you can more easily handle maintenance tasks, repairs, and tenant issues, allowing you to gain practical experience without feeling overwhelmed.

***Faster Learning Curve:*** Starting small allows you to learn the fundamentals of real estate investing at a manageable pace. You can familiarize yourself with the process of property acquisition, management, and resale without the complexities associated with larger projects. This hands-on experience will help you build confidence and expertise over time.

*Flexibility for Growth:* Beginning with a smaller investment provides flexibility for future growth and expansion. As you gain experience and confidence, you can gradually scale up your investments by acquiring additional properties or pursuing larger projects. Starting small allows you to lay a solid foundation for future success in real estate investing.

*Diversification:* Investing in a single-family home or condominium offers diversification benefits for your investment portfolio. Real estate investments have a low correlation with traditional financial assets like stocks and bonds, so adding a property to your portfolio can help spread risk and enhance overall diversification.

*Research Local Markets:* Research local real estate markets to identify areas with strong rental demand, favorable appreciation potential, and affordable properties. Look for neighborhoods with amenities like schools, parks, and public transportation that appeal to potential tenants or buyers.Researching local real estate markets is essential for identifying promising investment opportunities.

Understanding your local market is crucial. Let us explore why and how to research it effectively.

*Rental Demand:* Understanding rental demand is crucial for investors interested in rental properties. Research local demographics, employment trends, and population growth to gauge demand for rental housing. Look for areas with a stable or growing population, a high proportion of renters, and low vacancy rates to ensure consistent rental income.

*Appreciation Potential:* Assessing appreciation potential helps investors identify areas where property values are likely to increase over time.

Analyze historical price trends, market forecasts, and economic indicators to gauge future appreciation potential. Look for neighborhoods undergoing revitalization of urban development projects that could drive property appreciation in the long term.

*Affordability:* Consider the affordability of properties in the area relative to your budget and investment objectives. Research median home prices, rental rates, and affordability metrics to ensure properties are within your financial reach. Look for opportunities to invest in up-and-coming neighborhoods or emerging markets where property prices are still relatively affordable compared to established areas.

*Neighborhood Amenities:* Evaluate neighborhood amenities and quality of life factors that appeal to potential tenants or buyers. Look for neighborhoods with access to amenities such as schools, parks, shopping centers, restaurants, and public transportation.

Proximity to employment centers, schools, and major transportation routes can enhance the desirability of a property and attract tenants or buyers.

*Market Dynamics:* Understand the overall market dynamics in the area, including supply and demand trends, market competition, and regulatory factors. Research local housing market reports, real estate listings, and rental listings to gain insights into market conditions. Pay attention to factors like inventory levels, days on the market, and pricing trends to assess market competitiveness and identify investment opportunities.

*Local Regulations:* Familiarize yourself with local regulations, zoning ordinances, and landlord-tenant laws that may impact your investment strategy. Research rental regulations, property taxes, and licensing requirements to ensure compliance with local laws and regulations. Consult with legal and real estate professionals to navigate regulatory complexities and mitigate legal risks.

By thoroughly researching local real estate markets, investors can identify areas with strong rental demand, favorable appreciation potential, and affordable properties. This research lays the groundwork for informed investment decisions and maximizes the likelihood of success in real estate investing.

## Networking and Building Relationships

Networking is essential in real estate investing. Connect with real estate agents, property managers, contractors, and other industry professionals who can provide valuable insights, advice, and opportunities. Building relationships can open doors to potential investment deals and partnerships.

Networking plays a crucial role in real estate investing, providing valuable opportunities for learning, collaboration, and growth.

Why networking is essential and how you can leverage it effectively:

***Access to Opportunities:*** Networking allows you to connect with a diverse range of real estate professionals, including real estate agents, property managers, contractors, lenders, and investors. By creating connections with these people, you have access to significant options such as off-market transactions, property listings, and investment partnerships that may not be accessible via standard channels.

***Industry Insights and Advice:*** Networking gives a chance to learn from experienced experts and obtain insights into the local real estate industry. By engaging in discussions, By attending business events and participating in networking organizations, you may benefit from the knowledge and skills of others. Experienced investors, real estate agents, and property managers may give you useful information, suggestions, and best practices to help you negotiate the complexity of real estate investment.

***Partnerships and Collaborations:*** Networking opens the door to prospective partnerships and collaborations with other industry specialists. By creating strategic connections with real estate agents, property managers, or contractors, you may harness their talents, resources, and networks to boost your investment chances. Collaborating with others helps you pool resources, share risks, and access new markets, eventually enhancing your potential for success.

***Deal Sourcing and Referrals:*** Networking helps you grow your network of connections and sources for investment opportunities. By creating contacts with real estate brokers, wholesalers, and other investors, you boost your chances of obtaining recommendations for possible investment possibilities. Networking also helps you to get into the "grapevine" of the real estate sector, where word-of-mouth referrals and insider information may lead to profitable transactions.

***Building Credibility and Trust:*** Networking helps you develop credibility and build trust within the real estate sector. By actively engaging in networking events, sharing your experience, and giving help to others, you show your dedication to the sector and your desire to contribute constructively. As you create rapport and credibility over time, you become regarded as a respectable and trustworthy investor, which may lead to new possibilities and collaborations.

***Staying updated and Connected:*** Networking keeps you updated and connected to the latest developments and trends in the real estate market. By remaining connected with other professionals, attending industry events, and engaging in online forums or social media groups, you may stay current on market developments, regulatory updates, and upcoming possibilities. Networking also offers a support system of like-minded people who understand the problems and possibilities of real estate investment.

***Perform Due Diligence:*** Before making any investment, undertake extensive due diligence to examine the property's condition, market potential, and financial feasibility. This may entail evaluating the property, assessing similar sales, and reviewing rental revenue and spending predictions. Due diligence is a vital phase in the real estate investing process, helping investors examine the feasibility and possible dangers of a property.

Why due diligence is crucial and how you can execute it effectively:

***Property Condition:*** Assessing the condition of the property is vital to knowing its present status and possible remodeling requirements. Conduct a complete evaluation of the property, including its structural soundness, mechanical systems, and esthetic aspects. Identify any flaws or shortcomings that may need repairs or improvements, and estimate the related expenses.

***Market Potential:*** Evaluate the market potential of the property to evaluate its desirability to renters or purchasers. Research local market trends, rental rates, vacancy rates, and property appreciation rates to determine demand and supply dynamics. Consider aspects like location, neighborhood amenities, and closeness to schools, parks, and public transit when determining market potential.

***Financial viability:*** analyze the financial viability of the investment by analyzing revenue and expenditure predictions, cash flow analysis, and return on investment calculations. Obtain rental revenue and spending data from the seller or property management to analyze the property's income-generating potential. Factor in expenditures such as property taxes, insurance, maintenance, and property management fees to establish the property's net operating income and cash flow.

***Comparable Sales Study:*** Conduct a comparable sales study to estimate the fair market value of the property. Research recent sales of similar properties in the area to identify comparable properties and their selling prices. Consider factors such as size, location, condition, and amenities when selecting comparable properties and adjusting for differences to arrive at an accurate valuation.

***Legal and Regulatory Compliance:*** Ensure the property complies with all legal and regulatory requirements, including zoning ordinances, building codes, and rental regulations. Review property documents, permits, and inspection reports to verify compliance and identify any potential issues or violations. Consult with legal professionals or real estate experts to address any concerns and ensure a smooth transaction.

***Environmental and Title Issues:*** Investigate any environmental concerns or title issues that may affect the property's value or marketability. Obtain environmental assessments and title reports to identify potential risks such as contamination, easements, liens, or encroachments. Address any issues through negotiations with the seller or by obtaining appropriate insurance or mitigation measures.

***Take Action:*** Once you have done your research and identified a promising investment opportunity, don't hesitate to take action. Make an offer, negotiate terms, and move forward with the transaction. Remember that real estate investment is a dynamic and competitive business, so being decisive is vital.

Taking action is vital in real estate investment, particularly when you have spotted a great prospect. Why it is vital and important for you to take action, and how you should continue with confidence:

***Seizing Opportunities:*** In real estate investment, time is frequently essential. Once you have completed comprehensive research and selected a property that corresponds with your investment requirements and aspirations, it's crucial to move promptly to capture the opportunity. Delaying might result in lost opportunities or losing out to rivals who move quicker.

***Negotiating conditions:*** When making an offer on a home, be prepared to discuss conditions with the seller. Negotiation helps you to debate pricing, contingencies, financing conditions, and other aspects to create a mutually advantageous arrangement. Work together with your real estate agent or adviser to design a competitive offer that stands out while safeguarding your interests.

***Due Diligence Contingencies:*** When making an offer, consider including due diligence contingencies to protect yourself throughout the inspection and review process. These conditions enable you to conduct more inquiries into the property's condition, market potential, and financial sustainability before concluding the acquisition. Use this time effectively to check your original results and handle any problems that may emerge.

***Commitment and Confidence:*** Demonstrating commitment and confidence in your offer will help boost your position as a serious buyer. Sellers are more willing to accept bids from buyers who demonstrate real interest and preparedness to go ahead. Present yourself as a competent and dependable investor who is willing to follow through on the agreement.

***Adapting to Market Dynamics:*** Real estate markets are dynamic and may change swiftly. Be prepared to alter your approach and adjust your offer depending on market circumstances, seller response, and other pertinent considerations. Flexibility and agility are crucial to negotiating the complexity of the real estate market and capturing opportunities as they occur.

***Seeking professional direction:*** If you are confused about specific components of the deal or require direction, don't hesitate to seek counsel from real estate specialists, legal advisers, or financial experts. Experienced specialists can give useful insights, negotiate on your behalf, and ensure that your interests are safeguarded throughout the transaction process.

## Dynamics to enhance your chance of success in the competitive real estate market

*Check and adjust:* After purchasing a property, check its performance and make modifications as appropriate. Stay updated about market trends, rental demand, and property valuations to make educated choices about managing your investment portfolio.
Monitoring the performance of your investment property is critical for optimizing earnings and avoiding hazards.

*Here is why it is crucial and how you can efficiently manage your financial portfolio:*

*Maximizing Returns:* Regularly monitoring the performance of your investment property helps you uncover chances for improving income and lowering expenditures. By examining rental revenue, vacancy rates, and operational expenditures, you may discover areas for improvement and adopt strategies to increase cash flow and profitability.

*Mitigating Risks:* Monitoring your investment property helps you identify and address potential risks before they escalate. By staying informed about market trends, rental demand, and property values, you can proactively respond to changes in the market and mitigate risks such as declining property values, increased vacancy rates, or changes in regulatory requirements.

*Identifying Opportunities:* Monitoring market trends and property performance enables you to identify opportunities for growth and expansion within your investment portfolio. By staying informed about emerging market trends, demographic shifts, and investment opportunities, you can capitalize on favorable market conditions and strategically grow your real estate portfolio over time.

***Optimizing Management:*** Monitoring your investment property allows you to assess the effectiveness of your property management strategy and make adjustments as needed. By evaluating the performance of property managers, maintenance providers, and other service providers, you can ensure that your property is being managed efficiently and effectively to maximize returns and tenant satisfaction.

***Staying competitive:*** Keeping abreast of market trends and rental demand helps you stay competitive in the real estate market. By understanding tenant preferences, rental rates, and amenities that appeal to renters or buyers, you can position your property effectively to attract and retain tenants and maintain high occupancy rates.

***Adapting to Market Dynamics:*** Real estate markets are dynamic and subject to change, so it's essential to adapt your investment strategy in response to market conditions. By monitoring market trends and property performance, you can make informed decisions about buying, selling, or refinancing properties to capitalize on opportunities and mitigate risks in a changing market.

***Seeking Professional Guidance:*** Consider seeking advice from real estate professionals, property managers, or financial advisors to help you effectively monitor and manage your investment portfolio. Experienced professionals can provide valuable insights, analysis, and recommendations to help you optimize property performance and achieve your investment objectives

## Understanding the Basics of Real Estate Investment

Building a secure financial base is the cornerstone of thriving in real estate investment. This involves crafting a realistic budget that outlines your income and expenses. It is equally important to develop a strategy for managing debt effectively. This could involve paying down high-interest loans or utilizing debt strategically to leverage your investments. Finally, mastering cash flow management ensures you have the necessary funds to cover ongoing property expenses, taxes, and unexpected costs. By solidifying these financial fundamentals, you will be well-equipped to navigate the opportunities and challenges of real estate investing, ultimately propelling you towards your long-term financial objectives.

***Foundation for Success:*** Just like any other activity, a thorough grasp of the essentials builds the foundation for success in real estate investing. Knowing important ideas, terminology, and techniques helps you navigate the market with confidence and make educated judgments.

***Risk Management:*** Real estate investing has inherent hazards, but mastering the essentials helps you recognize and reduce these risks efficiently. By learning how to analyze property values, examine market trends, and manage funds, you may decrease the possibility of financial loss and increase possible rewards.

***Investment techniques:*** Real estate provides a range of investment techniques, from rental properties to fix-and-flip ventures to commercial buildings. Understanding the fundamentals lets you understand which tactics correspond with your objectives, resources, and risk tolerance, enabling you to adjust your strategy appropriately.

***Financial Literacy:*** Real estate investing demands financial literacy to assess transactions, acquire financing, and manage cash flow properly. Understanding topics like property value, financing choices, and return on investment helps you make informed financial decisions and improve the performance of your assets.

***Market Knowledge:*** Real estate markets are dynamic and susceptible to change, so being educated about market trends, demographics, and economic indicators is vital. Understanding the principles of real estate investing empowers you with the skills to understand market data, recognize opportunities, and modify your plan to meet market circumstances.

***Long-Term preparation:*** Real estate investing is generally a long-term enterprise involving patience, tenacity, and strategic preparation. Understanding the fundamentals helps you build a clear investment strategy, set reasonable objectives, and measure your progress over time, enhancing your chances of attaining long-term success in the market.

***Continuous Learning:*** Real estate investing is a continual learning process, and mastering the fundamentals is only the beginning. As you acquire experience and confront new problems, you'll need to consistently extend your knowledge, polish your abilities, and keep current with industry advancements to remain competitive in the market.

## Building a Strong Financial Foundation for Real Estate Investing

Assessing your financial condition is a key step before plunging into real estate investing. Here is an explanation of why it is necessary and how you can go about it:

***Understanding Your Financial Health:*** Assessing your financial condition requires taking stock of your present financial resources, commitments, and aspirations. This involves analyzing your income, assets, obligations, spending, and savings. Understanding your financial health offers you a clear view of your total financial status and helps you make educated choices regarding real estate investing.

***Determining Your Investment Capacity:*** Once you have a clear grasp of your financial condition, you can evaluate how much you can afford to invest in real estate. This entails evaluating your available resources, analyzing your risk tolerance, and selecting your investing objectives. Assessing your investing capacity helps you establish reasonable objectives and prevent overextending yourself financially.

***Evaluating Financing Choices:*** Real estate investing frequently demands large funds, so reviewing your financial status also entails examining your financing choices. This involves investigating mortgage programs, loan possibilities, and other financial alternatives to establish the most acceptable solution for your requirements. Understanding your financing alternatives helps you harness external cash to optimize your investment potential.

***Budgeting and Planning:*** Assessing your financial status requires setting a budget and financial plan for your real estate investing initiatives. This involves putting aside cash for property purchases, refurbishment charges, continuing expenses, and contingencies. Establishing a budget and financial plan helps you allocate resources efficiently and prioritize spending, and manage cash flow throughout the investing process.

***Managing Debt and Cash Flow:*** Evaluating your financial condition also entails managing current debt commitments and ensuring adequate cash flow to fund your investing activity. This may mean combining high-interest debts, refinancing current loans, or rearranging your finances to free up funds for investment objectives. Managing debt and cash flow properly helps you maintain financial stability and reduce the risks associated with real estate investing.

***Seeking Professional Guidance:*** Assessing your financial status might be difficult, so it's vital to obtain expert help from financial advisers, mortgage brokers, or real estate specialists. An experienced adviser can help you examine your financial status, research funding possibilities, and design a customized investment plan matched to your objectives and risk tolerance.

## Setting Realistic Goals for House Flipping

When it comes to effectively managing several property flips, setting objectives that are possible to achieve is a key component. Some things to think about while you are establishing your objectives are:

***Conditions of the market:*** It is important to pay special attention to the broad trends and present circumstances of the overall housing market. When it comes to deciding what kinds of properties to invest in and when to sell them, this will be of great assistance.

***Budget:*** Determine the amount of your investment and the frequency of your investments by doing an analysis of your financial resources and limits.

***Location:*** When searching for real estate, look for homes in regions that are in high demand and have the possibility for growth and development to occur.

Researching the sorts of individuals that are looking for homes in the market that you are targeting is an important part of the demographic research. Determine the kind of real estate that they are most interested in purchasing, and then direct your investment choices in accordance with that information. Conquering the fast-paced world of property flips requires laser focus and unwavering motivation. Here is where setting **smart** goals becomes your secret weapon:

***Specific and Measurable:*** Avoid vague aspirations like "make a lot of money." Instead, define clear, measurable goals like "secure financing within 30 days" or "complete kitchen renovation by [date] under budget." Tracking progress towards these specific milestones fuels confidence and keeps you on track.

***Attainable and Ambitious:*** Balance ambition with reality. Don't aim to renovate a complete fixer-upper in a month if you're a beginner. Set achievable goals that challenge you to stretch your skills while remaining realistic based on market conditions, your budget, and renovation expertise.

***Relevant and Time-Bound:*** Ensure your goals directly contribute to your overall flipping strategy. For example, aiming to "increase curb appeal by 15%" aligns with attracting buyers and potentially fetching a higher price. Assign deadlines to each goal to create a sense of urgency and prevent procrastination.

*Translating SMART Goals into Actionable Strategies:*

***Become a Market Master:*** Research your target area to identify undervalued properties with strong profit potential. Look for homes in desirable locations with cosmetic issues or outdated finishes that can be revitalized with cost-effective renovations. This approach maximizes profit potential while minimizing renovation costs.

***Budgeting Like a Boss:*** Craft a detailed budget that outlines renovation costs, holding costs (taxes, insurance), and your target profit margin. Do not just create it; actively monitor expenses against your budget. Identify areas for potential savings and adjust strategies as needed to stay on track financially.

***Renovation Roadmap to Success:*** Break down your renovation project into achievable milestones with target completion dates. This meticulous planning helps you stay organized, manage contractors effectively, and avoid project delays that can devour profits.

***Exit Strategy in Focus:*** Clearly define your ideal buyer profile (families, young professionals) and tailor your renovations to their preferences. This increases your chances of a quick sale at your desired price point. Consider strategic upgrades like modernizing kitchens and bathrooms or improving energy efficiency, which are highly sought-after features by today's buyers.

***Become a Renovation Ninja (Focus on Low-Cost Repairs):*** This aligns with the "achievable" aspect of SMART goals. Cultivate an eagle eye for identifying high-impact, low-cost repairs. Prioritize cosmetic fixes like painting, replacing outdated hardware, or sprucing up curb appeal with landscaping. Remember, potential buyers are often swayed by aesthetics. For plumbing or electrical work, solicit bids from multiple qualified contractors to ensure you're getting the best value.

***Craft Homes with Sizzle (Create Beautiful Homes):*** This aligns with the "relevant" aspect of SMART goals. Do not just renovate; renovate strategically! Conduct thorough research on current design trends and buyer preferences in your target area. Focus on renovations that enhance curb appeal, modernize kitchens and bathrooms—areas with a high return on investment—and improve functionality. Striking a balance between aesthetics and cost-effectiveness is key. Do not get carried away with high-end finishes if they will not translate to a significant increase in your selling price.

**Know Your Ideal Buyer (Target the Appropriate Buyers):** Understanding your target demographic is crucial for setting "relevant" and "Time-Bound" goals. Research demographics and buyer profiles in your chosen area. Are you targeting young families who need a safe and spacious backyard? Busy professionals seeking move-in-ready convenience? Tailor your renovations and marketing strategy to their specific needs and preferences. This can significantly impact how quickly you sell the property and the price you can command. For instance, focusing on energy-efficient upgrades might attract eco-conscious buyers who are willing to pay a premium.

**Budgeting Like a Boss (Stick to a Budget):** Budgeting aligns with the "measurable" aspect of SMART goals, and financial discipline is paramount for success. Create a detailed budget that factors in renovation costs, holding costs (taxes, insurance, interest), and your desired profit margin. Utilize tools like spreadsheets or project management software to meticulously track your expenses throughout the project. Identify areas for potential savings by comparing contractor quotes and exploring cost-effective materials without sacrificing quality. Adjust strategies as needed to ensure you stay within your budget and avoid profit-eating surprises.

By creating realistic objectives, you may boost your chances of success and optimize your earnings. Remember to consider market circumstances, demographics, finances, and geography while formulating your objectives. Hold yourself responsible and emphasize cost-saving methods that increase curb appeal and target the appropriate customer.

## Creating a Timeline

One of the keys to effectively managing several property flips is having a clear and detailed timetable in place. A timetable helps keep your projects on track, ensures that all essential work is performed, and helps you prioritize activities.

## Importance of Having a Timeline

A timetable helps you stay organized and on track, enhancing overall efficiency. When it comes to effectively managing several property flips, setting objectives that are possible to achieve is a key component. Some things to think about while you are establishing your objectives are as follows:

***Market circumstances:*** Pay careful attention to the housing market's present conditions and general tendencies. When it comes to deciding what kinds of properties to invest in and when to sell them, this will be of great assistance.

***Budget:*** Determine the amount of your investment and the frequency of your investments by doing an analysis of your financial resources and limits.

***Location:*** When searching for real estate, look for homes in regions that are in high demand and have the possibility for growth and development to occur.

Researching the sorts of individuals that are looking for homes in the market that you are targeting is an important part of the demographic research. Determine the kind of real estate that they are most interested in purchasing, and then direct your investment choices in accordance with that information.

## Master Timeline for Multiple House Flips

### *Pre-Acquisition (1-2 weeks before Week 1)*

1. Secure finance for the project (if required)

2. Identify and select prospective properties

## Week 1: Assessment and Planning

1. Conduct a comprehensive investigation of each property to establish the extent of work

2. prioritize repairs and improvements based on budget and market trends

3. Obtain quotations from contractors for significant remodeling tasks

4. Apply for appropriate permissions and schedule inspections

## Week 2-3: Demolition and Rough-In

1. Begin the destruction of undesired buildings or finishes

2. Start any structural repairs that are necessary

3. Rough-in plumbing and electrical systems

4. Order materials with lead times to prevent delays

5. Hire and schedule subcontractors for specific work (e.g., roofers, plumbers, electricians)

## Weeks 4-6: Building Envelope and Core Systems

1. Install new windows and doors

2. Complete roofing and siding repairs or replacements

3. Continue plumbing and electrical work (including fixture rough-in)

4. Install drywall and insulation

5. Weeks 7-8: Interior Finishes

6. Paint the inside and outside of the home

7. Install cabinetry and flooring

8. Complete installation of plumbing and electrical fittings

9. Schedule inspections for plumbing and electrical work

## Weeks 9-10: Final Touches and Turnover

1. Install appliances, countertops, and other finishes

2. Complete landscape and exterior renovations

3. Conduct a final cleaning and touch-up

## *Week 11: Listing and Sales*

1. Stage the home for showings to attract buyers

2. Final inspection and occupancy permit (if necessary)

3. Launch marketing activities (photography, listing on MLS, etc.)

4. Conduct open houses and property viewings
Week 12+

5. Sell the property and conclude the agreement

6. Use the earnings to support the next project or replenish reserves

## Key Considerations for Multiple Flips

*Phasing:* Staggering the purchase and refurbishment deadlines of multiple properties may aid with cash flow management and resource allocation.

*Communication:* Maintain clear communication with contractors, subcontractors, and your staff to guarantee a seamless workflow throughout all projects.

*Buffer Time:* Build buffer time in the schedule to cover for unanticipated delays or material shortages.

*Market Conditions:* Stay updated about market developments and change refurbishment plans or pricing tactics as appropriate.

## Leverage the Power of Outsourcing to Supercharge Your House Flips

In the fast-paced world of house flipping, efficiency is king. By strategically outsourcing tasks, you can streamline your operations, maximize profits, and elevate the quality of your flips.

Here is how outsourcing empowers you to become a house-flipping powerhouse:

### Sharpen Your Focus, Sharpen Your Profits

Imagine being able to dedicate more time to deal sourcing, negotiation, and the overall project strategy. Outsourcing frees you from the minutia of everyday tasks, allowing you to focus on the high-impact decisions that drive profitability. Think of yourself as the conductor of a renovation orchestra, ensuring everything runs smoothly without getting bogged down in playing every instrument.

***Cost Control Through Strategic Partnerships:*** While outsourcing might seem like an added expense, it can lead to significant cost savings.

*Here is the secret sauce:*

***Economies of Scale:*** Contractors often have established relationships with material suppliers, giving them access to bulk discounts that you might not be able to secure on your own. This translates to lower material costs for your project.

***First-Time Right Every Time:*** Experienced contractors complete tasks efficiently and avoid costly mistakes that can lead to wasted materials and rework. This translates to a more predictable budget and less stress throughout the renovation process.

***Expertise You Can Bank On:*** One of the most compelling benefits of outsourcing is the access to specialized knowledge and experience that seasoned contractors bring to the table. This ensures top-notch workmanship that adheres to building codes and avoids potential safety hazards or code violations that could lead to costly delays and rework down the road.

***Time is Money:*** In the world of house flipping, speed is often critical. By outsourcing tasks, you tap into the efficiency of experienced professionals who have the right tools and crews to complete projects quickly and effectively. This minimizes the time a property sits on the market, allowing you to sell it sooner and get your capital back in hand to fuel your next project.

***Adaptability is Your Superpower:*** The world of house flipping is full of surprises. Unexpected issues can arise, throwing a wrench into your carefully crafted timeline. Outsourcing allows you to adapt to these challenges with agility. Need a plumber on short notice to address a sudden leak? A reliable contractor can step in and keep your project on track. This flexibility gives you peace of mind and ensures you can address unforeseen circumstances without derailing your entire project.

## The Tasks Best Left to the Pros:

Here is a breakdown of specific tasks where outsourcing truly shines:

***Behind the Walls:*** Plumbing and electrical work are complex and require licensed professionals to ensure safety and avoid costly code violations. These systems are the lifeblood of a modern home, and entrusting them to experts guarantees a job well done.

***Solid Foundation, Solid Investment:*** Roofing and foundation repairs are not DIY projects. Leave these critical tasks to skilled professionals who can identify and address potential problems that could lead to major structural issues down the line, saving you from a potential money pit.

***Comfort is Key:*** A well-functioning HVAC (heating,ventilation,and air conditioning) system is essential for buyer comfort and adds significant value to a property. Hiring experienced technicians for installation and repair ensures optimal performance and avoids potential headaches for future homeowners.

***Showstopping Transformations:*** Kitchens and bathrooms are major selling points, so don't underestimate their impact. Skilled contractors can deliver high-quality renovations that will leave potential buyers wowed, translating into a higher selling price for you.

***Curb Appeal that Sells:*** First impressions matter, and professional landscaping and exterior improvements significantly enhance a property's value and visual appeal. Outsourcing these tasks ensures your flip boasts a stunning exterior that entices buyers to step inside and explore further.

# Building a Reliable Team

Building a successful home flipping company takes much more than simply purchasing and selling houses. To optimize your revenues and decrease your stress levels, you need to develop a trusted team of specialists that are knowledgeable, experienced, and devoted to your success. In this chapter, we will explore the necessity of having a dependable team, the features of an ideal team, and recommendations on developing a reliable team for your house-flipping company.

## Importance of Having a Reliable Team

House flipping is a difficult and demanding business that demands skill in several areas, such as real estate, finance, construction, and marketing. As a home flipper, you cannot handle everything by yourself, and you need a team of competent professionals to help you succeed. A trustworthy team will save you time, money, and hassles and guarantee that your homes are refurbished to the highest standards and sold quickly at the best possible price.

## Characteristics of an Ideal Team

An excellent crew for your house-flipping company should include the following characteristics:

***Experience:*** Your team members should have a track record of accomplishment in their respective professions and should be able to manage any problems that occur.

***Expertise:*** Your team members should have the essential skills and expertise to accomplish their responsibilities successfully and efficiently.

***Dedication:*** Your team members should be enthusiastic about their jobs and devoted to your success.

***Communication:*** Your team members should be able to communicate effectively with each other and with you to ensure that everyone is on the same page.

***Flexibility:*** Your team members should be able to adjust to changing conditions and be prepared to go above and beyond to get the task done.

## Building a Reliable Team

Building a trustworthy staff for your house-flipping company entails the following tips:

***Identify your duties and responsibilities:*** Before you start establishing your team, you need to identify your personal position and obligations as the home flipper. This can help you determine the talents and expertise you require from your team members.

***Network and recruit:*** To locate the best team members, you need to network and recruit from multiple sources, such as your personal contacts, industry organizations, online job portals, and social media.

***Interview and vet:*** When you have a list of possible team members, you need to interview and vet them properly to verify that they satisfy your standards and are a good fit for your team.

***Train and support:*** Once you have picked your team members, you need to give them the appropriate training, tools, and support to do their responsibilities successfully and efficiently. You also need to offer them clear comments and assistance to help them improve their performance.

***Check and assess:*** As your team members work on your home flipping projects, you need to check and analyze their performance often to ensure that they are meeting your expectations and reaching your objectives. You also need to offer them positive comments and appreciation to keep them motivated and interested.

## Prioritizing and Organizing Tasks

Flipping many residences at the same time may be a tough process. In order to keep on top of things, it is vital to prioritize and arrange work properly. Setting priorities and planning your tasks will help you stay focused on the important things that will directly affect your house flipping endeavors. Some of the important factors include;

1. It helps you manage your time effectively by breaking down activities into smaller, manageable components.

2. It reduces uncertainty and stress by giving a clear path for accomplishing activities within a predetermined period.

3. Increases productivity by minimizing distractions and maintaining a methodical approach to finishing work.

## *Tips for Prioritizing and Organizing Tasks*

1. Start with a full list of all the tasks that need to be performed, including deadlines.

2. Sort jobs depending on their priority level, urgency, and influence on the entire project.

3. Assign assignments to team members based on their skill set, availability, and workload.

4. Set attainable objectives for finishing activities and break down huge projects into smaller milestones.

5. Create a timetable that provides time for eventualities and unanticipated difficulties.

## Tools and Technologies that Help in Prioritizing and Organizing Tasks

1. Project management software: allows you to divide down projects into smaller components, assign them to team members, and monitor progress.

2. Task management apps: enable you to build to-do lists, set reminders, and get alerts for completed tasks.

3. Communication tools: facilitate smooth communication among team members and ensure everyone is on the same page.

4. Time tracking software: It helps you manage your team's productivity and track billable hours for each project.

5. Cloud-based storage: This allows you to save and share project-related documents and data with team members, regardless of their location.

Prioritizing and arranging work is a vital component of managing numerous property flips. By breaking down activities into smaller, manageable components and utilizing technology to automate and optimize your workflow, you can enhance productivity, keep on top of deadlines, and effectively manage many home flipping projects at the same time.

## Managing Finances

Managing funds correctly is vital to the success of many property flips. Without adequate financial management, the price of improvements and unanticipated expenditures may rapidly spiral out of hand, leaving flippers with little to no return. Here are some ideas on handling expenses for many property flips:

## importance of handling funds successfully

1. Minimizes the chances of unexpected costs

2. Helps keep track of spending and income

3. Ensures profitability and sustainability

4. Helps develop a solid financial basis for future initiatives

## How to handle expenses for several home flips

1. Create a comprehensive budget before commencing any remodeling job

2. Keep note of all costs, especially little ones such as paint and nails

3. Set up a separate bank account for each project to minimize confusion and keep financial information organized

4. Establish a contingency fund to cover unforeseen expenditures

5. Regularly examine and evaluate financial data to discover opportunities for improvement

6. Negotiate with contractors and suppliers for competitive rates and discounts

7. Avoid overpaying and needless costs by prioritizing upgrades that bring value to the property

8. Monitor market trends to make educated judgments regarding the time and price of the property sale

9. Keep investors and stakeholders updated about the financial state of the project.

## Helpful tools and software for managing money

1. Accounting software such as QuickBooks or Xero may help keep track of spending, earnings, and taxes

2. Project management software such as Trello or Asana may help keep track of appointments, deadlines, and to-do lists

3. Real estate applications such as Zillow or Redfin may assist in studying the home market and estimating property prices

4. Budgeting applications such as Mint or Good budget may help manage costs and measure progress toward financial objectives

Effective financial management is a vital component of effectively managing several property flips. By making a precise budget, keeping track of all spending, setting up a contingency fund, and leveraging helpful tools and software, flippers may reduce the risks of unexpected expenses, boost profitability, and create a solid financial foundation for future projects

## Communication

Effective communication is vital when conducting many house flips. Good communication reduces misunderstandings, delays, and errors, all of which may damage a project.

1. Start by writing a project communication plan that defines who needs to communicate with whom and how often.

2. Have weekly meetings with the team to assess progress, goals, and any issues that develop.

3. Set precise expectations for contractors, including timeframes, budgets, and quality requirements.

4. Listen to comments and concerns from team members and contractors, and address them immediately and respectfully.

5. Use technology to assist collaboration, such as project management software, group chat programs, and online file sharing tools.

6. Avoid communication failures by being proactive, responsive, and genuine. Provide regular updates to stakeholders, such as investors and real estate agents, to keep them informed and interested.

7. Document critical communication in writing, such as contracts, emails, and task lists, to avoid misunderstandings and protect yourself legally.

Essentially, excellent communication is about developing trust and relationships with your personnel and contractors. By being an excellent communicator, you can assure that everyone is on the same page and working towards the same purpose.

# Protecting Yourself: Liability Insurance

The Property Brothers make it seem so simple. These well-known "fixer-upper" shows portray a repair and flip as being simple and completed in less than an hour, but in reality, they are more complicated. However, any experienced property investor will tell you that this is not the truth. Flips always come with an element of danger. And no matter how sure an investment seems, there is always the chance for things to go wrong. Therefore, you need to be insured.

That being said, insurance for home flippers may be a subject that is tricky to understand and brings up a lot of questions: How much protection do you need? What sort of insurance do you need? And how much is that going to cost you? If you have any queries concerning repair and flip insurance, we have got you covered (no pun intended).

In this chapter, we are going to address all the concerns you may have regarding the insurance side of home flipping so you can feel comfortable with whatever your repair and flip project may throw at you. Let's get into it.

## Is insurance required when flipping houses?

Do not even contemplate getting into a repair and flip project without insurance! As we indicated, there are a plethora of things that might go amiss when flipping properties. Not convinced? Here are several extremely possible things that may go wrong:
- Your home might burn down
- A contractor could be injured.
- Your property could be vandalized
- Building gear and supplies could be taken

So why risk it? The insurance products we will examine in this chapter safeguard your property and personal assets and, ultimately, provide you with peace of mind.

## What types of insurance coverage do you need for house flipping?

Flipping residences needs a unique form of insurance coverage. A standard homeowner's insurance policy will not protect you. Moreover, it is also dubious that your usual insurance broker—the one you use for your property or car—would provide the sort of coverage you are wanting.

This is because typical insurance brokers see house-flipping as 'high risk'. Furthermore, they are not meant to safeguard empty or renovated houses.

The unique sorts of insurance you require for repairs and flips are:
1. Dwelling Policy
2. Builder's Risk Policy
3. General Liability Umbrella

**What is a dwelling Policy:** A dwelling policy for an empty building that's under renovation is to safeguard against direct and physical harm to

the property. As a flipper, these unplanned occurrences may happen at any step of a repair or flip. And insurers view it that way too.
Vacant or remodeled homes are considered a greater risk since they're more prone to vandalism, water damage, or arson.

***What is a Builder's Risk Policy:*** A builder's risk insurance coverage is something you'd have to purchase if you're carrying out a structural renovation of a house. It covers immediate, physical damage to a property during the building process. It is worth remembering that certain housing insurance does not cover restoration or supplies. If that's the case, it's important you add a 'builder's risk rider' to your policy.

***What is a General Liability Umbrella Policy:*** A general liability insurance policy is implemented to provide protection against bodily injury occurring on the premises. However, this coverage does not apply to your general contractors or the personnel you employ. With all of your policies, you need to remember that all properties are distinct, and yours will have its own specific needs. To determine the coverage you require, consult your real estate dream team, which includes an experienced private money lender, a dependable real estate agent, and your insurance company.

## How Much Protection Do You Need From Insurance?

Insurance coverage is not created equal. Therefore, it is worth calculating how much coverage you need for your investment home. Otherwise, you run the risk of having too little or too much insurance.

There are two main alternatives for insurance coverage:

***Basic form coverage:*** This offers coverage for all of the reasons stated in your policy; all other causes of damage are excluded. This sort of coverage may save you upwards of 30%, but ensure you examine these exclusions. Common exclusions include theft, sleet or snow, and water damage.

***Special form coverage:*** This sort of form offers coverage for all sources of loss, except for those mentioned as exclusions in your policy. Exclusions to be aware of include sewage & drain backlogs, earthquakes, floods, and deliberate damage.

You also have the choice of two kinds of settlement techniques that affect your insurance rates and the amount you may collect in the case of a loss.

1. Actual Cash Value
2. Replacement Cost Value

***Actual cash value:*** Actual cash value coverage settles claims based upon the property's value in it's current condition. Actual cash value is calculated by taking today's replacement value and deducting depreciation to account for the property's age and wear-and-tear. Actual cash value places you in a bad situation since you may not be able to recuperate all of your money that you would need to completely re-build the property.

***Replacement Cost Value:*** Replacement cost value coverage compensates claims based on the amount of money it would take to replace your damaged or destroyed house with the same or a comparable property in today's market. It is vital to remember that the replacement cost value only covers the value of the property, not the value of the land.

In general, at the very least, you want to secure adequate insurance coverage to cover the amount you paid for the house (minus the lot value) plus the amount spent on the property for upgrades. However, in the case of a catastrophic loss where you lose the whole structure, you will either have to entirely re-build the property at full replacement cost or sell off the lot to another investor for them to re-build.In such circumstances, you will want to obtain enough coverage to pay for the replacement of the property or enough coverage to avoid a loss if you have to liquidate the lot.

**What is the cost of insurance on a flip?**

This question is a little more difficult to answer than the others. This is due to the fact that fees differ significantly and are determined by several factors, including:
• Geographical location
• The worth of your property
• The amount and kind of coverage you opt to have

## When should you get insurance for your flip?

Like most things in life, it is better not to put off insurance for home flipping until the last minute. Otherwise, you may miss something vital. It is advised that you start contacting insurance brokers and requesting quotes as soon as your house is under contract. As soon as you take ownership of the property, it's your financial duty. Therefore, you don't want to get caught out because you delayed purchasing insurance. Additional Measures for Safeguarding Your Interests in Real Estate Flipping Besides getting your property insured, there are a few other precautions you can take when flipping properties to protect yourself.

Firstly, flippers should sign the contract, receive their insurance coverage, and deal with finance via an LLC. An LLC safeguards your personal assets and assures that you're not personally accountable for anything going. wrong with your property. The truth is that most private money lenders will not give you money until you set up an LLC (Limited Liability Company) or a S corp (a corporation that chooses to pass through corporate profits, losses, deductions, and credits to its shareholders for federal tax purposes).

Furthermore, it is critical to surround oneself with a qualified real estate team, as was previously mentioned in passing. , it is critical to surround oneself with a qualified real estate team, as was previously mentioned in passing. Flips may be hazardous when handled in the incorrect manner. Moreover, they need you as an investor to wear a number of different hats and utilize your best judgment within a range of specialties. Being able to draw on professionals will guarantee that all the choices you make are completely informed.

## Importance of Liability Insurance for House Flippers

Liability insurance is of essential relevance for home flippers owing to the specific hazards involved with their area of business. Here's why liability insurance is necessary for those active in flipping houses:

***Property Damage Coverage:*** House flipping entails considerable remodeling and construction work, which may raise the risk of unintentional property damage. Liability insurance offers coverage for property damage incurred during remodeling operations, guaranteeing that house flippers are financially covered against unanticipated losses to the property or surrounding buildings.

***Bodily Injury Protection:*** Renovation projects may be in dangerous settings, with dangers of slips, falls, and other mishaps for workers and visitors. Liability insurance gives protection against bodily injury claims originating from incidents on the property. This coverage applies to injuries incurred by contractors, subcontractors, and anybody else who may be present on the construction site.

***Legal responsibility Coverage:*** House flippers may bear legal responsibility for accidents or damages caused by third parties owing to carelessness or harmful conditions on the property. Liability insurance offers coverage for legal defense expenses, settlement payments, and judgments obtained against the house flipper in lawsuits stemming from property-related occurrences.

***Contractual Obligations:*** House flippers typically get into contracts with property owners, investors, lenders, and subcontractors, which may involve liability insurance obligations. Having liability insurance in place not only meets contractual duties but also communicates professionalism, dependability, and financial responsibility to business partners and stakeholders.

***Protection Against Lawsuits:*** House flipping projects can attract legal disputes from various parties, including property owners, tenants, neighbors, and regulatory authorities. Liability insurance acts as a safeguard against costly lawsuits and litigation expenses, protecting house flippers from financial ruin in the event of legal disputes or claims arising from their business activities.

***Risk Management Tool:*** Liability insurance serves as a crucial risk management tool for house flippers, helping them mitigate the financial risks associated with their operations. By transferring potential liabilities to an insurance provider, house flippers can protect their personal assets, business interests, and future earnings from the adverse consequences of property-related incidents.

## How to Find Affordable Insurance Option

Finding economical insurance choices is vital for home flippers to manage expenses efficiently while maintaining proper coverage. Some of the techniques that help home flippers locate inexpensive insurance options include:

***Compare Multiple Quotes:*** Obtain quotes from various insurance carriers to evaluate coverage choices and costs. Shopping around helps home flippers uncover competitive prices and select insurance products that give the greatest value for their unique requirements.

***Bundle plans:*** Consider combining insurance plans with the same carrier to take advantage of multi-policy savings. Many insurance providers offer discounts for combining homeowners insurance, liability insurance, and other coverage types into a single policy, resulting in cost savings for house flippers.

***Opt for higher deductibles:*** Choosing greater deductibles might help cut insurance prices, since house flippers bear more financial responsibility for claims before insurance coverage kicks in. Evaluate the trade-off between cheaper premiums and greater out-of-pocket expenditures to identify the most cost-effective deductible amount for your budget and risk tolerance.

***Seek Specialized Insurance:*** Look for insurance carriers who specialize in coverage for real estate investors or home flipping operations. These insurers may provide bespoke insurance solutions created expressly for the unique risks connected with flipping properties, sometimes at more attractive prices than standard insurers.

***Evaluate Coverage Limits:*** Review coverage limitations and alter them depending on your risk exposure and financial resources. While appropriate coverage is vital, home flippers should avoid over-insuring properties and liability risks beyond their real requirements.

Assess your risk profile and coverage needs to identify suitable policy limits that balance protection and cost.

***Improve Risk Management Practices:*** Implement risk management methods to limit insurance claims and show proactive risk reduction to insurance carriers. This may involve maintaining safe work conditions, complying with construction rules and safety requirements, and employing quality control procedures to limit the possibility of accidents, injuries, and property damage.

***Maintain a Good Credit Score:*** Insurance companies generally evaluate credit scores when deciding rates, since those with better credit scores are seen as lower-risk consumers. Maintaining a strong credit score by managing debt responsibly and paying payments on time helps house flippers qualify for reduced insurance rates and more favorable conditions.

***Review policy discounts:*** Inquire about potential discounts and incentives that might help cut insurance prices. Common discounts may include claims-free discounts, safety and security discounts, loyalty discounts for long-term policyholders, and savings for installing protective equipment like smoke detectors and security alarms.

# Finding the Deal: Where to Look for Properties

There are numerous methods to uncover rehab offers in our industry today. In today's heated and competitive market, it's becoming more difficult to discover offers via conventional means, like the MLS. In this session, we will cover the distinction between 'on-market' & 'off-market' offers and analyze the most effective techniques to currently locate bargains in today's market.

On Market Vs Off Market Deals

There are two main approaches to locating discounts in today's market:

1. 'On-Market' Deals
2. 'Off-Market' Deals

***On Market transactions:*** 'On-market' refers to transactions that are posted on the MLS (Multiple Listing Service). 'On-Market' transactions are advertised online and are readily accessible to any buyer who has access to the

MLS. Since 'On-Market' bargains are so freely available, there is significantly more competition. If you are looking for properties on the MLS, you are competing against other investors, but you are also competing against 'retail purchasers' as well. This certainly pushes up costs and makes it much more difficult to discover offers that can earn a significant profit. Off deals. 'Off-Market' deals relate to transactions that cannot be located on the MLS marketplace. These bargains are harder to uncover but have less competition, so you may acquire houses at a discount. Finding 'Off-Market' offers involves more 'hustle', but frequently results in the greatest deals that bring the highest profit potential.

What is the MLS, and how may it be utilized to identify bargains in today's market? Then we will explore the most popular and effective techniques to find 'Off-Market' offers.

## MLS (Multiple Listing Service)

As noted earlier, the MLS is the internet listing marketplace that sellers utilize to offer their homes for sale. If you are selling your house, you obviously want to put your property on the MLS since that is where all of the retail buyers go to browse for properties. However, if you are searching for possible opportunities, the MLS is quite competitive, and you will probably find it tough to identify rehab projects that can create a decent return.

***Recent History of the MLS:*** Back in 2008–2012, the market was over-saturated with foreclosures from the financial crisis, so you could readily discover distressed houses and rehab transactions at a lucrative price.

***Today's Market:*** Flash forward to today's market, and most of the foreclosure inventory has dried up. Today's market inventory cannot keep up with buyer demand, and houses are getting numerous bids above the asking price.

Obviously, engaging in bidding battles with other investors & retail purchasers and over-paying for property is not a prescription for flipping success. Remember, you earn money when you purchase! The MLS is not completely useless in today's market. Although you may not find many deals on the MLS, it is a good idea to keep an eye on it so you have a pulse on the market.

Sign-up with a local brokerage to receive daily MLS notifications of new property listings in your market, so you can keep an eye on market inventory and market competition.

***Some of the insurance obligations are;***

***Driving for dollars***

Driving for dollars' is one of the finest tactics for locating discounts, but it costs time, effort, and petrol money. 'Driving for dollars' is the practice of driving about areas and seeking out houses that seem distressed or abandoned and that might be owned by a seller who is eager to sell.

*Here are some symptoms you should watch for:*

1. Overgrown vegetation
2. Bad driveway
3. Deteriorating roof
4. Junk or rubbish in yard
5. Property for Rent
6. For Sale by Owner

Once you discover a property that qualifies, put a business post card at the door or scribble down the address and send a letter to the property owner. You can often discover the property owner's name on the county recorder's website. From there, you could investigate their contact details. Again, this technique involves time, effort, & money, but in order to locate 'off-market' offers that nobody else knows about, you will have to do things that nobody else wants to do. You do not want to be driving all over town looking for deals!

## *The Enduring Significance of Real Estate Investment Groups: Networking and Opportunity Acquisition*

The pursuit of success in the dynamic world of real estate investment hinges on the cultivation of a robust professional network. Real Estate Investment Groups (REIGs) serve as a cornerstone in this endeavor, providing a platform for investors to forge invaluable connections with a diverse range of industry specialists. These gatherings transcend mere meetings; they transform into fertile ground where mutually beneficial relationships blossom.

Imagine a vibrant space teeming with real estate agents, wholesalers, and fellow property rehabilitators, all residing within your local market. REIG meetings provide the unique opportunity to connect with each of these individuals, transforming them from names on a page to trusted allies. Real estate agents, possessing an intimate understanding of the local market, can become your eyes and ears, keeping you apprised of prime listings before they hit the mainstream. Wholesalers, acting as facilitators, can unveil hidden gems—properties ripe for rehabilitation and brimming with potential, by delivering them directly to your attention. And finally, fellow property rehabilitators, sharing the trenches of the investment landscape, evolve into a source of shared knowledge and strategic insights.

Identifying REIGs tailored to your investment goals is a remarkably simple feat. Social media platforms like Facebook and Meetup furnish intuitive search functions, enabling you to locate groups operating within your specific geographic area Notably, REIG meetings and online forums hosted by these platforms often serve as a launchpad for discussions spearheaded by wholesalers. These industry veterans generously share their expertise, illuminating details of potential rehabilitation projects that might otherwise remain undiscovered.

Beyond the realm of forging connections, REIGs often cultivate a spirit of camaraderie and collaboration. My experience paints a vivid picture of local REIGs as havens for dedicated investors, united by a fervent desire to witness their communities flourish. Members demonstrably embody a commitment to shared success, readily sharing their accumulated wisdom, hard-won experience, and time-tested strategies with their peers. By actively engaging in stimulating conversations and fostering connections with fellow property rehabilitators and flippers within the community, you unlock the potential to unearth invaluable tactics employed to secure properties at advantageous prices.

In essence, REIGs function as catalysts, propelling investors towards achieving their financial aspirations. Through active participation in REIG activities, you gain access to a network teeming with qualified professionals, each interaction enriching your knowledge base and deal-making prowess. As you delve deeper into the REIG community, a constant stream of lucrative investment opportunities comes into view, propelling you toward a future brimming with financial triumphs.

Do not be scared to put yourself out there! You will meet all types of fantastic contacts at local real estate events or meetings that may help you uncover bargains and share insider secrets in your local market. 'Your network is your net worth!'.. Real estate brokers and local agents could be another source for probable 'off-market' renovation deals.

In circumstances where a seller has a troubled home and is facing foreclosure, divorce, or death in the family, the seller sometimes doesn't want to deal with the inconvenience of putting their property on the MLS. In these cases, the seller may call a real estate agent to arrange an off-market purchase with a local rehabber, who may provide cash for the home and close swiftly.

This is where your networking & connections with local agents are key!

## *Wholesalers*

A wholesaler is a local investor who specializes in discovering distressed, 'off-market' businesses. The advantages of employing a wholesaler are that they are performing the 'hustle work' to obtain the 'off-market' discounts. They are leveraging their time, resources, and marketing money to uncover the 'off-market' treatment offers for you. For their efforts to locate the bargain, they collect a modest wholesale fee (usually 5% of the purchase price).

Perform a Google search of local wholesalers in your city (ex: Kansas City Real Estate Wholesalers), and Google should be able to discover a list of the big wholesalers in your region. Most wholesalers will have a website set up with a list of current inventory and offer you the choice to subscribe to their mailing lists. You may also locate wholesalers at your local REIG meetings, Facebook groups, or Meetups.

Find out which wholesalers operate in your 'farm market', identify yourself, and outline your purchasing requirements for your rehab transactions.

Always review the wholesaler's project numbers, 'With a Grain of Salt' because oftentimes after repair, values are repaired and costs are underestimated.

Always perform Your due diligence Check to see if the wholesaler's deal is a deal!

Auctions Foreclosure, estate, or private auctions are wonderful chances to acquire properties at reduced rates.

## *Sheriff's Sales:*

Your first step to purchasing a property at a sheriff's sale is to do your homework. Most foreclosure auction listings are issued by the county several weeks before the sale in the press or on their county courthouse website. If the Sheriff Sale information is not easily accessible online, contact your local town or county courthouse for further information. Once you obtain the list of Sheriff Sales in your local county, choose the properties in your market that suit your purchasing requirements and go visit the property in person to examine the condition of the property. Unfortunately, due diligence on Sheriff's Sales might be tough since you can only see the property from the street and won't be able to assess the inside condition. If possible, peer in windows, or attempt to acquire the 'inside scoop' from neighbors. When in doubt, simply assume the inside of the property is a complete gut.

Before auction day, pick the highest bid you are willing to make for the property. When a bidding war develops, don't get upset and overbid for the property. Stick to your highest offer price, and if you are outbid, walk away and go on to the next house!

## *Estate Sales*

Estate auctions are used to liquidate the assets of a family or an estate, often after a death, but they may also be utilized for downsizing, relocating, divorce, or bankruptcy. Similar to Sheriff Sales, estate sales are often publicized in the press, but you should also check local Auctioneer's websites. In fact, I would encourage you to subscribe to your local auctioneer's websites so you may obtain news of new estate sale events in your region. The positive thing about estate sales is that you will typically be able to tour the property to evaluate the property's condition before the auction, so you may make a comprehensive study of the property to choose your best offer.

Most auctioneers demand that the successful bidder deposit 5-10% of the purchase price as an earnest money deposit. Also, be careful to examine the auctioneer's conditions since they will normally charge a 10% 'buyer's premium'.

So if you purchased a house for $100,000, your total purchase price would be $110,000!

## Exploring Different Strategies And Sources for Finding Properties

Flipping real estate has been an extremely popular investment technique in recent years due to the fact that it offers the potential for higher profits. The success of this investment, on the other hand, is contingent upon a number of different elements, the most important of which is the identification of the appropriate property in the appropriate location. In the year 2023, it is anticipated that the real estate market will be very competitive, and it may be a challenging endeavor for any investor to locate the ideal house to flip.

In this chapter, we will be exploring the numerous methods that investors might use in order to locate possible properties that will result in big profits. Furthermore, we will also highlight the ideal regions to concentrate on while looking for houses to flip, including neighborhoods that are on the rise and markets that are now seeing a growing demand.

The practice of flipping real estate is a well-known financial technique that has the potential to generate substantial profits. The key to being successful in home flipping, however, is to locate the appropriate houses to invest in and to do so in the appropriate locations. As of 2024, the following is a list of the top ten tactics for discovering houses to flip, as well as the best regions to concentrate your search:

***Online Real Estate Marketplaces:*** Websites such as Zillow, Redfin, and Realtor.com are excellent locations to begin your search for houses that are currently available for purchase in your region. These sites allow you to search for homes based on particular parameters, such as price, location, and number of bedrooms, making it simpler to locate suitable flip properties. Focus your search on places with a rising population, low unemployment rates, and increasing property prices.

***Real estate agents:*** Working with a local real estate agent may be a helpful resource for identifying houses to flip. Real estate agents have access to MLS (Multiple Listing Service) databases, which are updated in real-time and feature extensive information about homes for sale. Ask your real estate agent to concentrate on locating homes in up-and-coming communities or places undergoing renovation.

***Foreclosure Auctions:*** Foreclosure auctions are an excellent method to identify houses to flip since these properties are generally priced below market value. You may obtain information about foreclosure auctions in your region via the local county clerk's office or internet sites such as Foreclosure.com.

***Networking:*** Building a network of real estate investors, contractors, and real estate agents will help you stay informed about prospective flip properties. Attend local real estate investing clubs, join online forums and social media groups, and engage with other real estate professionals to develop your network.

***Direct Mail Campaigns:*** Direct mail campaigns are a proven approach to creating leads and identifying houses to flip. You may run direct mail campaigns to home owners in locations where you are interested in flipping houses, offering to acquire their properties for cash.

***Tax Sales:*** Properties with overdue property taxes may be liquidated during tax sales. These homes might be a wonderful chance for flipping, since the owners are frequently keen to sell fast to avoid more penalties and interest on their unpaid taxes. You may get your area's tax sales information at the local county treasurer's office.

***Estate Sales:*** Properties being sold as part of an estate sale might also be a wonderful chance for flipping. These homes are generally offered below market value and may be a smart investment if they are in excellent shape and situated in a desired neighborhood. You may obtain information about estate sales in your region via local newspapers and internet sites such as EstateSales.net.

***Bank-owned homes:*** Banks regularly sell homes they have acquired via foreclosures, and these properties may be a fantastic chance for flipping since they are generally priced below market value. You may get information about bank-owned homes in your region from the local bank or through internet sites such as RealtyTrac.com

***Neighborhood Drives:*** Take a drive around the communities you are interested in flipping houses in and seek out properties that are in need of improvements and renovations. Focus on neighborhoods with a high proportion of aged properties, homes with delayed upkeep, and residences with outmoded architecture.

***Contact Private Sellers:*** You may look for homes on social media or by advertising that you are interested in acquiring properties in certain locations. Private sellers may be a useful source for identifying off-market assets that may not be accessible via standard means.

There are various ways to discover houses to flip, but by applying these top 10 tactics, you may boost your chances of finding the perfect property at the appropriate price. It's also crucial to examine each home and the surrounding community before investing.

As a real estate investor, knowing the local real estate market, the demographics of the area, and the future development plans will help you make educated judgments about where to invest. By evaluating characteristics such as crime rates, school districts, accessibility to amenities, and property prices, you may select the ideal locations to concentrate your search for flipping houses.

Therefore, let's dig into some of the things to consider when studying a property and its surrounding area before investing and discuss the essential variables to consider when looking for the finest communities to invest in when flipping houses in 2024.

***Focusing Your Flip Search:*** Targeting the Right Neighborhoods. When it comes to identifying the finest area to concentrate your search for houses to flip in 2024, some of the items to consider include the following:

• Up-and-coming areas with a rising population and increasing property values: These neighborhoods are generally distinguished by the inflow of young professionals and families who are drawn to the area's inexpensive housing, amenities, and proximity to employment hubs. As more individuals come into the community, property prices tend to climb.

• regions experiencing rehabilitation or gentrification: These regions may have been previously ignored or witnessed a drop in property prices, but are now witnessing a comeback in attention and investment. Revitalization initiatives may involve the rehabilitation of historic houses and structures, new construction, and the inclusion of amenities that make the neighborhood more desirable to purchasers.

• neighborhoods with a high concentration of aged property in need of updates and renovations: These neighborhoods generally feature houses and structures that were developed many decades ago and are in need of modernization or repairs. Investors might acquire these houses at a cheaper price point and refurbish them to boost their value and appeal to purchasers.

• places with low unemployment rates and a developing economy: These places tend to have a stronger demand for homes as individuals come to the area for work possibilities. This may lead to higher property prices, especially in places with a limited supply of homes.

• Areas with high foreclosure rates and low property values: While high foreclosure rates might be an indication of economic turmoil, they can also provide chances for investors to acquire homes at a cheaper price point and repair them for resale.

• Properties situated near government jobs: These places may have a more steady value, particularly during recessions. Government occupations may be a wonderful sign of a stable work market in a location, since these positions generally offer steady employment throughout economic downturns. This stability may help sustain property prices, especially in locations with a large concentration of government workers.

• Neighborhoods with a high concentration of aging populations: These places may give investors chances to acquire houses from older homeowners wishing to downsize or move into assisted living. With the correct repairs and modifications, these houses may be appealing to younger purchasers who may be searching for more inexpensive housing alternatives.

Now that we have extensively reviewed the numerous aspects to consider while looking for houses to flip, let's dig into the top 5 cities that are positioned for house flipping success in 2024. Based on statistics from trustworthy sources such as Realtor.com, the National Association of Realtors, Redfin, FRED, World Population Review, Balance Everything, and CNBC, these cities have exhibited robust property markets, economic development, and a variety of prospects for home flipping. So, if you're going to invest in real estate in 2024, these locations should be at the top of your list when examining prospective investment possibilities in real estate in 2024.

## 5 Best Cities To Flip Houses 2024

Flipping properties may be a very satisfying and successful financial strategy. If you are researching regions to invest in fix-and-flip projects in 2024, here are five cities worth looking into.

1. Chicago, IL
2. Cleveland, OH
3. Fayetteville, NC
4. Jacksonville, FL
5. Philadelphia, PA

**Chicago, IL**
One of the top cities for fix-and-flip projects is Chicago. With a typical house value of roughly $285,000, Chicago provides diverse real estate possibilities, catering to varied budgets and interests.

With properties lasting roughly 49 days on the market, inventory moves pretty swiftly, showing that demand is still alive. In November 2023, there were 9,369 houses for sale, which isn't enough to match the demand. However, the supply and demand indices weigh substantially in favor of local investors, meaning flippers should be able to take on projects quicker and sell for bigger profits.

**Cleveland, OH**

Cleveland is another place for investors to look into in 2024. With a strong reputation for healthcare and research businesses, Cleveland has fueled demand for homes. An inflow of students and professionals drawn by the rise of healthcare occupations and educational possibilities adds to an increasing requirement for accommodation.

That said, the rising demand has obviously outweighed the 2,963 available properties for sale in November 2024. Additionally, real estate is a coveted commodity in Cleveland, with an inexpensive median house value of $98,000. As a consequence, properties are only on the market for roughly 49 days, which should offer investors peace of mind that their fix-and-flip projects will see plenty of demand.

## *Fayetteville, NC*

Fayetteville, North Carolina, has positioned itself as a desirable site for home flipping in 2024. With a typical property value of roughly

$200,000, the city presents a more inexpensive housing environment, particularly compared to its prominent neighboring city, Raleigh. In consequence, Fayetteville has experienced increasing demand from those wanting to avoid higher property prices in Raleigh's real estate market.

Growing demand in this region has led to properties spending fewer days on the market. With an average of 41 days on the market, properties in Fayetteville sell rather rapidly, reflecting demand that may aid local investors. In turn, this implies a great climate for house flippers to acquire, repair, and sell houses, maximizing earnings in a shorter time period.

### *Jacksonville, FL*

Another successful city for home flipping in 2024 is Jacksonville, Florida. With a typical property value of roughly $295,000, the city provides a broad selection of homes at moderate rates. This makes it an appealing market for fix-and-flip investors searching for advantageous pricing.

The average number of days residences spend on the market is roughly 50, which shows that properties are being sold swiftly. This implies investors have a greater likelihood of quicker investment returns. Jacksonville's low unemployment rate and relatively high median family income also indicate a stable economic climate. This may stimulate demand for real estate transactions, improving the possibility of selling refurbished houses.

### *Philadelphia, PA*

Philadelphia is becoming another fantastic area to invest in fix-and-flip houses. The typical house valuation in this popular city is roughly $214,000, giving an ideal starting point for investors. Additionally, properties sell rather rapidly, with an average of 43 days on the market. This fast-paced climate enables flippers to purchase, refurbish, and resell residences very rapidly.

Additionally, another reason that makes Philadelphia a famous city to invest in is the foreclosure rate of 0.75, which is pretty high.

However, this greater rate means a considerable volume of houses flowing through the market, giving additional opportunity for investors to obtain properties at costs below market value.

## Identifying potential investment opportunities

Identifying possible investment possibilities is key to successful real estate investing. Here are some guidelines to help you locate excellent investing opportunities:

Market Research: Conduct extensive market research to discover places with great growth potential, suitable demographics, and high demand for rental properties or house purchases. Analyze market trends, economic data, population growth, employment rates, and infrastructural advancements to locate attractive investment markets.

***Networking:*** Build connections with real estate agents, property managers, investors, and other industry experts who may give useful insights and opportunities. Attend networking events, join real estate investing clubs, and participate in local communities to develop your network and keep updated about new investment possibilities. Online Listings and Auctions: Utilize online real estate listings platforms, auction websites, and property databases to look for investment properties. These systems enable you to select properties based on location, price range, property type, and other parameters, making it simpler to locate prospective investment options that match your individual needs.

***Drive or Walk Around:*** Take a proactive approach by driving or strolling around communities to locate homes with potential for investment. Look for dilapidated or neglected properties, empty lots, and properties with "For Sale" signs or foreclosure notifications. A physical examination of neighborhoods helps you to analyze the condition of homes and uncover prospective investment possibilities that may not be posted online.

***Direct Mail Marketing:*** Implement direct mail marketing campaigns to target property owners who may be interested in selling their properties. Send individualized letters, postcards, or flyers to property owners in target locations expressing your interest in acquiring properties for investment objectives. Direct mail marketing may provide leads and possibilities that may not be accessible via regular means.

***Wholesalers and Bird Dogs:*** Establish contacts with wholesalers and bird dogs that specialize in identifying off-market bargains and distressed homes. Wholesalers seek distressed homes, negotiate purchase contracts, and then transfer these contracts to investors for a fee. Bird dogs look for possible investment opportunities and suggest them to investors in return for a finder's fee or commission.

***Property Auctions and Foreclosures:*** Attend property auctions, foreclosure sales, and tax lien auctions to uncover inexpensive investment properties. Auctions give the possibility of acquiring properties below market value but require significant due diligence and planning. Research auction processes, bidding regulations, and property liens to find prospective investment possibilities and prevent expensive blunders.

Real Estate Investment Trusts (REITs): Consider investing in Real Estate Investment Trusts (REITs), which are publicly listed businesses that own and manage income-producing real estate assets. REITs provide investors exposure to various portfolios of real estate assets, including residential,
commercial and industrial assets, without the requirement to physically acquire and manage buildings.

*Facilitating Mutually Beneficial Relationships: A Framework for Effective Networking*

***More Than Handshakes:*** Building a Network for Real Estate Success (This highlights the depth of relationship required for successful networking.)

Networking opportunities may have disappeared off most of our calendars during the epidemic, but it's time to get back in the practice of going out there and meeting new people. Whether you adore the notion of mixing with strangers or feel a little apprehensive at the prospect of making cold contacts, networking may make connections materialize.

In the fast-paced world of real estate, networking isn't just a buzzword—it's a crucial cornerstone of success. Real estate is an industry driven by connections, and it's crucial to consistently feed your pipeline with fresh leads. How you engage with customers, other agents, and community members may dramatically affect your trajectory in the business. For agents looking to grow their reach and deepen their impact, understanding the art of networking is important.

## Why Networking Matters for Real Estate Professionals

A large network may provide referrals, up-to-date market information, cooperation possibilities, and client leads. It is about developing a network of relationships that you can tap into and contribute to. Approaching networking events with a receptive mindset fosters positive outcomes. You never know how your relationships can assist your bottom line, so with an eye toward efficiency and a mentality open to possibilities, let's delve into how to make the most of these encounters.

In a competitive real estate market, how can you differentiate yourself and become a memorable choice for clients?

**Small Gifts:** A conventional tactic with a twist. While business cards are the norm, combining them with a tiny memento may create a lasting impression. Steer clear of products new connections may regard as irritating waste and instead aim for functionality like pencils or snack bars. Bonus points if you can tie your own brand to your marketing item!

**Tell a Story:** Everyone has a sales pitch. Instead, present a compelling, client-centric success story that displays your abilities and passion. It's a wonderful approach to connecting emotionally with your audience.

**Use Technology:** Augmented reality (AR) business cards, QR codes that lead to a virtual tour of a property, or a digital portfolio may set you apart. Embrace technology to deliver a deeper, more engaging experience.

## Where to Find Networking Opportunities

Initially, you will want to cast a broad net and investigate various networking possibilities. However, with time, be judicious about which are useful compared to those that may be omitted. Consider searching in the following areas:

***Chamber of Commerce:*** An excellent resource for local professionals. Joining your local Chamber of Commerce provides you access to community events, seminars, and introductions to local companies. Since many communities have more than one, check out those that provide free meetings before investing in a membership.

***Networking Groups:*** Organizations such as BNI (Business Network International) provide organized venues to meet people across numerous disciplines. These provide a place to communicate recommendations and develop cooperation. Remember to be cautious of the time commitments required in each individual group, as some have attendance and referral requirements while others are more free-form.

***Real estate organizations:*** Become an active member of national or regional real estate organizations. Not only do they supply learning tools, but they also conduct events, seminars, and conferences that are perfect for networking.

***Online Platforms:*** Sites like LinkedIn may be valuable tools. Join real estate-specific groups, engage in debates, and share your thoughts.

Local community activities: Sponsor or participate in community activities. From local fairs to charity drives, these events are ideal for meeting new customers and creating a local presence.

## Strategies to Enhance Your Networking Game

***Be Genuine:*** While it's crucial to market your brand, networking isn't simply about sales. Genuine partnerships are founded on mutual respect and interest. Engage in interactions without necessarily anticipating a commercial consequence. Approach networking as a long-term strategy rather than short-term lead creation.

***Listen Actively:*** Networking is not a monologue. Listen to comprehend, not merely to answer. You will be astonished at the ideas and possibilities you may uncover by just listening. Ask questions and urge new contacts to share more so you demonstrate involvement.

Regular Follow-ups: Met someone at an event? Send them a thank-you letter, share an item of interest, or even a simple "It was great meeting you" message. This ensures your connection remains valuable and relevant.

***Educate While You Network:*** Instead of selling services, try delivering value. Host a brief webinar on house-staging, give insights on market trends, or provide ideas on home upgrades. By doing so, you present yourself as an expert on the topic.

Collaborate: Networking isn't simply about boosting your customer base. Connect with experts whose services correspond with yours - interior designers, landscapers, or mortgage brokers. Such contacts might lead to reciprocal recommendations and cooperation.

Stay updated: The real estate market is dynamic. Stay current with the newest trends, news, and legislation. It will offer you new talking topics and help you exhibit your passion for the field.

***Set clear goals:*** Before attending any networking event, determine what you want to accomplish. Whether it's meeting prospective customers, discovering cooperation possibilities, or learning something new, having defined objectives can direct your interactions and make them more successful.

Networking in the real estate industry is about developing true, long-term connections. It's a constant process of learning, sharing, and developing together. With the correct methods and a genuine attitude, networking can be the cornerstone of a prosperous real estate business. Remember, every relationship is a potential door to opportunity—ensure you have the correct key!

# Doing Your Homework: Due Diligence

## *Evaluating Potential Risks and Challenges*

It is essential for real estate investors to do rigorous due diligence in order to evaluate the feasibility of possible investment opportunities and the dangers associated with them. The following is an example of how you can carry out thorough due diligence:

***Property Inspection:*** Begin by assessing the property completely to determine its condition and identify any issues that may require repairs or modifications. To undertake a comprehensive evaluation of the property's structural integrity, mechanical systems, and general condition, it is recommended that you hire a highly skilled house inspector. Perform a title search to verify ownership of the property and discover any current liens, encumbrances, or legal difficulties that may impair the property's title. To safeguard yourself against the possibility of title flaws or ownership conflicts, you should get title insurance coverage now.

Analysis of the Financials Conduct an analysis of the financial components of the investment, including the property's expenses, the potential for rental revenue, and the predicted cash flow. In order to determine whether or not the investment is profitable, it is necessary to compute important financial indicators such as the capitalization rate, the cash-on-cash return, and the return on investment (ROI)

**Market Analysis:** Investigate local market conditions, including supply and demand dynamics, rental market trends, and property appreciation rates. Evaluate comparable sales data and rental comps to estimate the property's market worth and potential for appreciation.

Legal and regulatory compliance: Ensure that the property conforms with all relevant laws, rules, and zoning ordinances. Verify permits for any modifications or enhancements made to the property, and assess compliance with building codes and environmental rules.

***Environmental Assessment:*** Conduct an environmental assessment to detect any possible environmental dangers or pollution concerns related to the property. Obtain an environmental site assessment (ESA) to examine the property's environmental hazards and responsibilities.

***Insurance Coverage:*** Review your insurance choices to guarantee enough coverage for the property. Obtain insurance policies for property, liability, and any other coverage necessary to defend against property-related risks and liabilities.

***Contract study:*** carefully study and negotiate the details of purchase agreements, leasing agreements, and other legal papers linked to the investment. Seek legal advice to ensure that contract conditions are fair and advantageous, as well as to resolve any potential legal problems or concerns.

***Due Diligence Contingencies:*** Include due diligence contingencies in purchase contracts to allow an option to perform more research and inspections before concluding the acquisition. Use this opportunity to address any problems or concerns identified throughout the due diligence process.

***Professional Assistance:*** Consider engaging experts such as real estate agents, lawyers, accountants, and property inspectors to aid with the due diligence process. Their experience and counsel may help you identify potential dangers, negotiate advantageous conditions, and make informed investment decisions.

By completing extensive due diligence, real estate investors may reduce risks, find opportunities, and make educated investment choices that match their financial objectives and risk tolerance. investment, the time and effort to do extensive due diligence is vital for long-term success in real estate investment.

## Conducting thorough property research

Investing in real estate, whether buying, selling, renting, or leasing, requires a keen understanding of not just the property itself, but also the intricate web of factors influencing its value and marketability. This guide empowers you to navigate the crucial processes involved in conducting in-depth property research, equipping you with the knowledge to make informed decisions in the dynamic real estate landscape.

***Unveiling the Neighborhood:*** Laying the Groundwork. Your journey begins with meticulously exploring the neighborhood's demographics. This includes age distribution, household income levels, education levels, and family composition. By analyzing this data, you gain valuable insights into the property's target market: who are the potential renters or buyers? Understanding this demographic makeup helps you assess the property's overall attractiveness.

***Safety and Security:*** Safety is paramount. Analyze crime data for the area to determine its security. Lower crime rates are often associated with desirable communities, potentially impacting property values positively. A safe neighborhood fosters a higher quality of life for residents and can translate to a higher return on investment. Properties in areas with lower crime rates tend to attract more potential buyers, leading to increased competition and potentially higher selling prices.

***Educational Landscape:*** For families, the quality of local schools is a top priority. Evaluate the school systems, as strong districts can significantly influence demand and raise property prices in the area. Conversely, a neighborhood with underperforming schools might see lower property values due to decreased demand, particularly from families with children.

***Convenience and Amenities:*** Consider the proximity of the property to amenities such as parks, shopping centers, restaurants, and public transportation, and recreational facilities. Easy access to these facilities enhances the quality of life for residents and contributes to the property's overall appeal. A property close to desirable amenities like parks and green spaces can command a premium price compared to one in a more isolated location, especially for families or health-conscious renters/buyers.

## Navigating Market Trends: Charting Your Course

***Historical Insights:*** Gain valuable perspective by reviewing historical data on property sales, price trends, inventory levels, and market activity within the area. Analyzing historical trends allows you to identify patterns that might influence future property values. Understanding these historical fluctuations allows for more informed investment decisions and can help you identify potentially undervalued properties. For example, if you notice a consistent upward trend in property values in a particular neighborhood over the past five years, it might indicate a promising area for long-term investment.

***Current Market Snapshot:*** Stay informed by monitoring current market indicators such as median house prices, days on the market, and inventory levels. This information helps investors gauge market conditions and identify potential opportunities or challenges. Having a pulse on the current market allows for strategic decision-making, whether you're a buyer looking for a good deal or a seller aiming to maximize your return. A seller in a buyer's market with high inventory levels might need to adjust their listing price to attract interest, while a buyer in a seller's market with low inventory may need to act quickly and potentially offer above the asking price to secure a property.

***Future Outlook:*** Consider expert predictions, real estate market surveys, and economic projections to anticipate future market trends. Understanding potential shifts in supply and demand, interest rates, and economic conditions allows for informed investment decisions and strategic planning. By factoring in future market forecasts, you can make proactive decisions that align with your long-term investment goals. For instance, if economic projections suggest a potential recession on the horizon, you might choose to delay purchasing a property until the market stabilizes.

## Comparative Analysis: Equipping Yourself for Valuation

***Comparable Sales:*** Establish the property's market value by reviewing recent sales data for similar properties in the surrounding area. Look for comparable properties in terms of size, location, condition, and features. Analyze their selling prices to develop a baseline for appraisal. Having a clear understanding of comparable property values strengthens your negotiating position, whether you're a buyer making an offer or a seller setting a listing price. As a buyer, knowing the fair market value of a property helps you avoid overpaying, while a seller with a realistic understanding of comparable sales prices can price their property competitively to attract potential buyers.

***Property Feature Parity:*** Analyze the features and amenities of similar properties to estimate their relative worth. Properties with comparable features, renovations, or amenities may command similar prices in the market. This goes beyond just square footage; consider upgrades like modern kitchens, finished basements, or energy-efficient appliances that can add value to a property.

***Location Variables:*** Evaluate location-specific factors such as closeness to schools, transit, retail, and job areas. Homes in attractive locations or communities with easy access to amenities and job opportunities may fetch higher prices than identical homes in less desirable places. Conversely, properties situated near environmental hazards or industrial zones might see a decrease in value.

***projections:*** Consider economic projections, real estate market surveys, and expert predictions to anticipate future market trends. Understanding expected changes in supply and demand, interest rates, and economic circumstances may have an impact on investment choices and strategy.

***Property Feature Parity:*** Analyze the features and amenities of similar properties to estimate their relative worth. Properties with comparable features, renovations, or amenities may command similar prices in the market. This goes beyond just square footage; consider upgrades like modern kitchens, finished basements, or energy-efficient appliances that can add value to a property.

***Location Variables:*** Evaluate location-specific factors such as closeness to schools, transit, retail, and job areas. Homes in attractive locations or communities with easy access to amenities and job opportunities may fetch higher prices than identical homes in less desirable places. Conversely, properties situated near environmental hazards or industrial zones might see a decrease in value.

## *Assessing Rental Potential (if applicable):*

***Rental Rates:*** Research local rental rates for similar homes to determine prospective rental revenue. Consider aspects such as property size, condition, location, and amenities when evaluating rental prices.

***Vacancy Rates:*** Evaluate vacancy rates in the region to estimate rental market demand and competitiveness. Lower vacancy rates imply strong demand for rental properties and may promote increased rental revenue.

***Tenant Demographics:*** Consider the demographics of possible renters, such as age, income, and lifestyle choices, when determining rental possibilities. Understanding the target market helps tailor the property to meet the renter's demands and preferences.

## Property Condition:

***Inspection:*** A thorough inspection by a qualified professional is crucial. Look for signs of wear and tear, malfunctions, or outdated equipment that may require repair or replacement.

***Cosmetic Condition:*** Evaluate the cosmetic condition of the property, including interior finishes, flooring, paint, and fixtures. Cosmetic upgrades may boost the property's attractiveness to renters or purchasers and raise its market value.

## Financial Analysis:

**Acquisition Costs:** Calculate the entire acquisition costs, including the purchase price, closing charges, inspection fees, and other expenditures related to obtaining the property. Understanding the total cost of purchase helps establish the property's affordability and potential return on investment.

*Financing choices:* Explore financing choices such as mortgages, private loans, or cash purchases to establish the most cost-effective financing approach. Compare interest rates, periods, and fees to find the best financing solution for your investment objectives.

*Running expenditures:* Estimate continuous running expenditures such as property taxes, insurance premiums, maintenance charges, utilities, and property management fees. Understanding the recurring expenditures associated with property ownership helps estimate cash flow and profitability.

*Financial indicators:* Calculate important financial indicators such as cap rate, cash-on-cash return, and return on investment (ROI) to analyze the property's investment potential. These measurements give insights into the property's profitability and help compare investment prospects.

## Legal due diligence:

***Title Search:*** Conduct a title search to verify ownership of the property and identify any current liens, encumbrances, or legal difficulties that may impair the property's title. A clear title is necessary for transferring ownership and receiving financing for the property

***Property papers:*** Review property papers such as deeds, surveys, and easements to verify they are correct and up-to-date. Verify property borders, access rights, and any limitations that may affect the property's usage or development.

***Regulatory Compliance:*** Ensure the property conforms with local zoning restrictions, construction standards, and environmental regulations. To avoid legal issues or infractions, obtain permits and authorization for any planned modifications or upgrades.

## Understanding Neighborhood and Market Trends

*Identifying emerging neighborhoods and up-and-coming areas*

One of the most crucial parts of successful real estate investment is recognizing growing communities and up-and-coming locations. This demands a deep awareness of the local market as well as the wider economic and demographic factors that are driving the area. By keeping ahead of these trends, investors may position themselves to take advantage of opportunities before they become generally recognized and to optimize their returns on investment.

**Look for indicators of growth and development:** Growth and development are two of the most important indicators of an expanding neighborhood. This can take many forms, ranging from new building and restoration projects to the establishment of new companies and facilities. Investors should pay attention to these development signals and determine whether they are likely to persist over the long run. For example, if a new shopping mall is being developed in a certain location, it may imply that the population is rising and that there is demand for more retail space.

***Consider demographic trends:*** Another key thing to examine when determining growing communities is demographic change. This covers aspects such as population growth, age distribution, and income levels. Investors should search for places where the population is rising, especially among younger age groups, since this might imply a thriving and active community. Similarly, locations with higher average salaries may be more desirable for investors since they are likely to have more discretionary money to spend on housing and other facilities.

***Assess the local market:*** In addition to these general tendencies, investors should also evaluate the local real estate market in depth. This involves looking at criteria such as property valuations, rental rates, and vacancy rates. By knowing the local market, investors may discover regions where there is great demand for homes and where prices are expected to grow over time. This may also allow investors to discover regions where there may be opportunities to acquire discounted houses and generate substantial profits through repair and resale.

***Compare various alternatives:*** When evaluating growing communities and up-and-coming places, it is vital to examine many possibilities and analyze their respective strengths and shortcomings. This can include looking at numerous neighborhoods within a single city or comparing other cities or regions. Investors should examine variables such as accessibility to job hubs, transit choices, and the availability of amenities such as parks and retail centers. Investors may select the locations that are most likely to deliver the highest returns on investment by analyzing a variety of possibilities.

***Consider dealing with a local real estate agency:*** Finally, investors may want to consider dealing with a local real estate agent who has knowledge of the regions they are interested in. A local realtor may give significant insights into the local market, including knowledge on planned development projects, local zoning rules, and other issues that may affect the value of a property. They may also enable investors to navigate the purchasing and selling process and find possibilities that may not be well recognized.

Overall, locating new communities and up-and-coming locations is a vital element of successful real estate investment. By keeping ahead of the trends and studying the local market in depth, investors may uncover chances to create great returns and construct a lucrative portfolio over time. Whether working with a local agency or completing their own research, investors should approach this procedure with care and thoroughness in order to optimize their chances of success. Some of the trends in understanding a neighbourhood include:

## Market Trends

Understanding market trends in real estate requires studying many aspects that affect the dynamics of buying, selling, and investing in properties. Here's a basic breakdown:

***Supply and demand:*** Supply refers to the number of residences available for sale in a specific market.
***Demand:*** represents the number of purchasers seeking houses in the same market.

***Trend Analysis:*** Observing if supply is exceeding demand (buyer's market) or demand is outstripping supply (seller's market).


## Pricing Trends

***Price Appreciation:*** Examining whether house values are growing, declining, or stable over time.
***Comparative Analysis:*** Comparing current pricing to historical data to discover patterns.

## Market Activity

***Days on Market (DOM):*** tracking how long properties normally stay listed before being sold.
***Sales Volume:*** Analyzing the number of transactions happening during a specific time.

## Mortgage Rates

***Impact on Affordability:*** Understanding how variations in mortgage rates influence purchasers' buying power.
***Trend monitoring:*** observing whether rates are growing, dropping, or maintaining steady.

## Market Segmentation

***Luxury vs. Entry-Level:*** Recognizing variances in market dynamics between luxury houses and entry-level residences.
***Urban vs. Suburban:*** Understanding Variances in Market Patterns Between Urban, Suburban, and Rural Locations.

## Regional and local factors

***Economic Indicators:*** Considering local economic aspects such as employment growth, income levels, and industry developments.

***Regulatory Environment:*** Assessing how zoning restrictions and development policies affect the market.

***Trends:*** Observing population growth and migration trends to predict housing demand.

## Evaluating potential risks and challenges

When considering possible risks and problems in real estate investing, it's vital to evaluate several elements that might affect your investment. Here is a basic technique for assessing these risks:

## Market Risks

***Market Volatility:*** Real estate markets may undergo variations in property prices owing to variables including economic circumstances, interest rates, and investor mood. These swings might influence the profitability of investments.

***Economic Downturns:*** During recessions or economic slowdowns, demand for properties may decline, leading to extended holding periods or difficulties in selling properties at targeted prices.

***Regional Factors:*** Local economic circumstances, employment patterns, and regulatory changes may greatly affect property prices and investment returns in certain places.

Property-Specific Risks:

***Physical Condition:*** Properties may have structural difficulties or need extensive care, which may raise remodeling costs and reduce overall profitability.

***Location:*** The neighborhood where a property is situated might impact its appeal and value. Factors such as crime rates, school quality, and proximity to amenities might impact investment returns.

***Title difficulties:*** Legal challenges or encumbrances on the property's title might lead to delays in the selling process or unanticipated fees for addressing title difficulties.

## Financial Risks

***Leverage:*** While leveraging may boost gains, it also raises the risk involved with borrowing. Rising interest rates or unforeseen costs may make it hard to pay debt commitments.

***Cash Flow:*** Rental properties depend on continuous rental revenue to fund expenditures such as mortgage payments, property taxes, and maintenance charges. Vacancies or non-payment by renters could have a negative impact on cash flow.

*Market liquidity:* Properties may take longer to sell in sluggish markets or during economic downturns, reducing liquidity and consequently delaying the realization of gains.

## Legal and regulatory risks

*Zoning restrictions:* Properties must conform with municipal zoning laws and land use restrictions, which may prohibit certain forms of development or land use.

*Tenant regulations:* landlords must conform to regulations regulating tenant rights, eviction processes, and fair housing policies. Violations of these laws might result in legal battles and financial fines.

*Liability Exposure:* Property owners may be held accountable for accidents or damages that occur on their property. Adequate insurance coverage and risk management measures are needed to limit liability concerns.

## Environmental Risks

***Contamination:*** Properties situated in locations with environmental dangers, such as pollution or soil contamination, may pay remediation expenses or suffer legal obligations.

***Natural catastrophes:*** Properties in locations prone to natural catastrophes, such as hurricanes or earthquakes, are subject to hazards of property damage and interruption of operations.

## Management Risks

***Tenant Turnover:*** High tenant turnover rates may result in vacancies and additional expenditures associated with locating new tenants and preparing units for occupancy.

***Property Management:*** Effective property management entails resolving maintenance problems, addressing tenant complaints, and maintaining compliance with legislation.

Inadequate management may lead to property depreciation and tenant discontent.

## *Exit Strategy Risks*

*Market timing:* timing the sale of a property is crucial to maximizing earnings. Selling in a depressed market or in adverse economic circumstances may result in lower sales prices and lower profitability.

*Market circumstances:* Changes in market circumstances, such as oversupply or adjustments in buyer preferences, may affect the availability of buyers and the pace at which properties sell.

# Renovating for Profit: Adding Value to the Property

Your property is a potent instrument that you have at your disposal for the purpose of accumulating money if you are a homeowner. The value of your property may be greatly increased by making an investment in renovations, which will enable you to take advantage of the highest possible return on investment. In the event that you are considering selling your home or just wish to increase its value, the following are some helpful suggestions for increasing the value of your property through improvements.

***Prepare with a Purpose:*** Before beginning any kind of renovation job, it is very necessary to have a plan that has been well considered. Take into account your objectives, costs, and timetable. Research the market to determine the features and enhancements that are in high demand. For instance, kitchen and bathroom modifications, energy-efficient solutions, and outdoor living areas are commonly sought after by purchasers. Tailor your improvements to meet the tastes and demands of prospective purchasers, ensuring that your investment generates the highest returns.

***Focus on curb appeal:*** Because first impressions are so important, you should begin by working to improve the curb appeal of your home. Make investments in improving the front door, painting the outside, and landscaping the exterior. You will be able to attract prospective buyers and add value to your house by maintaining an exterior that is both visually attractive and well-maintained. Don't forget the importance of a beautiful front yard in establishing a lasting effect.

***Upgrades to the Kitchen and Bathrooms:*** The value of your house may be greatly increased by renovating your kitchen and bathrooms. These rooms are sometimes referred to as the "heart" of a house, and these are the places that purchasers focus their attention on the most. Consider updating appliances, worktops, cabinets, and fixtures. Modern, practical, and visually beautiful kitchens and bathrooms will appeal to prospective purchasers and improve your property's valuation.

*Energy Efficiency:* In today's ecologically sensitive society, energy efficiency is a crucial selling point. Consider investing in energy-efficient renovations like solar panels, LED lighting, insulation, and double-glazed windows. These upgrades not only cut utility expenditures but also boost the overall value of your house. Potential buyers are increasingly valuing sustainability, and an energy-efficient house may set you apart from the competition.

*Open Floor Plans:* Modern house purchasers frequently choose open, breezy areas that promote a smooth movement between rooms. If your house has a more conventional layout, consider eliminating non-load-bearing walls to create open floor designs. This will not only make your house seem more spacious but also correspond with modern design trends. Consult with a professional contractor to guarantee structural soundness and required permits before starting with any big improvements.

***Outdoor Living Spaces:*** In Australia's environment, outdoor living spaces are very attractive. Enhance your property's value by developing pleasant outside spaces such as decks, patios, or even a planted garden. Install utilitarian facilities like outdoor kitchens, fire pits, or sitting spaces. These expansions enhance the living area of your house, giving chances for leisure and enjoyment. Potential purchasers will enjoy the adaptability and lifestyle advantages that come with well-designed outdoor spaces.

***Seek Professional Advice:*** While DIY (Do It Yourself) improvements might reduce expenses, it's crucial to realize your limits. Certain renovations may need professional knowledge, such as structural alterations, electrical work, or plumbing upgrades. Hiring professional builders and tradesmen guarantees that your improvements are executed to a high degree, according to safety laws. Additionally, working with a real estate agent or property valuer may give significant insights into which upgrades would generate the maximum returns in your local market.

## Essential Renovations and Improvements

After you acquire a house to flip, the hard labor starts. Renovation is one of the most crucial tasks in home flipping. You need to improve the property's worth so that you can sell it for more than you paid for it. But you don't want to remodel everything without a strategy. It's vital to concentrate on improvements that add exceptional value. In this chapter, we are going to look at some of the greatest ROI improvements when you are flipping a house.

*Kitchen renovations and improvements:* If there is one location in a house you want to pay extra attention to when considering home improvements, it's the kitchen. Start by searching for cheap modifications that can be done without re-doing the whole room. Here are some suggestions to get you moving in the right direction:

• Repaint cabinets instead of replacing them (this might save a few thousand dollars).

• Install a composite countertop instead of granite or marble (this might save a few hundred bucks).

• Upgrade to energy-efficient appliances. Be careful to choose ones with verified claims, however.

• Replace outdated doorknobs and handles on sinks.

• Upgrade faucets. A sleek contemporary faucet is a wonderful little addition for most kitchens.

One crucial thing to keep in mind during this process is: don't over-improve a house. Remember, you want to be on par with the neighboring houses and earn a profit. Investing too much money and working into a flip is nearly as terrible as not doing enough. Balance is your best friend. Replace everything that is old and worn. Kitchens are a heavy traffic area in most abodes, so you want everything to seem fresh. Appliances are a vital aspect of every kitchen as well. Commercial appliances in excellent condition may be a crucial selling element for many purchasers. Thus, it's a great investment if you want to improve your property's value.

**Bathroom renovations and improvements:** Next, and you probably could have predicted this one, we have bathrooms. Bathrooms feature various pricey components that greatly change their worth. The most economical way to update a bathroom is by replacing its fixtures. A matching towel rack, faucet, door hinges, showerhead, and door handle may make the room seem a lot different (not to mention more contemporary). New medicine cabinets and new paint are also fantastic options. Painting will crop up numerous times in this essay. The reason for it is that it's an economical option to immediately add value and enhance aesthetics.

**Flooring:** If you need to replace the flooring in the house, hardwood is typically the finest alternative. Buyers normally anticipate it, generally enjoy how it feels and looks better than other choices, and are frequently prepared to pay extra for houses with it. Carpet, owing to its price and comfort, may be a preferable alternative for bedrooms or a basement. However, it's ideal to be as consistent as you can with flooring. Thus, hardwood should cover the bulk of the home. Even factoring in carpet's cheaper initial expenses, many statistics favor hardwood flooring, and that counts when you're attempting to earn a profit. According to Alex Biyevetskiy, a home renovation specialist, new hardwood flooring may add up to 2.5% to the selling price. The National Wood Flooring Association reports that 90% of real estate brokers think houses with hardwood flooring sell for more. Hardwood flooring may be able to improve your bottom line more than other forms of flooring. Hardwood's durability is a crucial aspect of its appeal as well. This form of flooring has a longer lifetime than other alternatives and can tolerate more wear and tear.

**Painting:** While we have previously discussed it for certain aspects of the house, painting needs its own section, too. It's one of the most economical and greatest ROI jobs you can perform while flipping a property. It helps the house seem nicer and adds value. Old paint that's flaking is evident right away when someone examines a property. Thus, the contrary is also true. Fresh, fresh paint is something prospective buyers will notice and appreciate, and stylistic accents like an accent color may boost the perceived worth of the property even more. Painting the inside and outside of the house is a cornerstone in the "flipping homes 101" repertoire. Painting the home's exterior is something that will pay big returns when you want to sell.

Lighting

Warm, welcoming lighting provides a warm ambiance that helps make a house seem like home. Most shoppers will instantly recognize when the lighting is excellent. It's not something most of us consciously think about until it's visibly off, yet it has a huge influence on our impression of a property. Windows have a role in how illumination is perceived in a house. Large front windows that allow in early sunshine or a pleasant glow in the later hours are a sought feature and help give the property a new appearance. Features like dimmer switches enable users to regulate emotions in a place. This may add value to a house. Another item worth noting here is LED bulbs. These energy saving gadgets rise in popularity every year since they're ecologically beneficial and fantastic for illuminating areas.

**Curb Appeal:** Do not overlook the "first impression" of the home you're attempting to sell. The more lovely a home appears from the outside, the more likely people are to want to view the interior. Imagine pulling up to your property for the very first time. What would be your honest, immediate reaction? If the response doesn't inspire confidence, you've got work to do. You can't show off the fantastic changes you've made inside a home if no one wants to stroll past the front of the property. Don't make this mistake. Things like installing a stone pathway, fresh mulch, or pruning bushes shouldn't be disregarded. These aren't costly overhauls, yet they can make a tremendous impact. Here are some tips for curb appeal modifications to boost home value when flipping:

• Add New Plants: Time and location will have an influence on your possibilities. However, an appealing flower bed with tiny trees, shrubs, potted plants, and vibrant flowers may liven up your home in no time.

• Get Rid of Weeds: A guaranteed way to harm your curb appeal is a yard overrun with weeds.

• Mow the grass: A well-kept front yard dramatically boosts curb appeal.

- Use Driveway Sealer: It's not going to break the bank, and you're going to have a much-improved driveway.

- Sweep: Getting rid of debris on pathways, the driveway, and around the front door or inviting entry adds cleanliness and charm.

## Budgeting and Managing Renovation Costs

Transforming a property for a successful flip hinges on meticulous planning from the outset. This meticulousness extends to both the renovation itself, demanding skillful project management to keep things on track, and the financial aspect, requiring unwavering cost control. By carefully orchestrating these elements, real estate enthusiasts can navigate the flipping process with confidence, maximizing their return on investment and mitigating potential risks.

## Importance Of Budgeting And Managing Renovation Costs

Managing remodeling costs and budgets is critical for various reasons. Firstly, it helps investors keep financial control throughout the project. By regularly monitoring spending, investors may uncover cost overruns or possible savings, making changes as required to keep within the authorized budget.Moreover, precise budget management helps investors make educated judgments regarding project scope, material selections, and design features. It guarantees that the remodeling matches the planned vision and market expectations while maximizing the return on investment.

Additionally, monitoring the budget fosters openness and responsibility. It helps investors communicate efficiently with contractors, suppliers, and other team members, ensuring everyone is on the same page on project expenses and financial aims.

## Effective Budgeting and Management Strategies:

Savvy real estate investors leverage several strategies to tighten their grip on remodeling budgets during property flips. These approaches empower them to maximize profits and minimize financial risks, paving the way for a successful renovation and flip.

**Establish a Detailed Budget:** Begin by preparing a complete budget that includes all projected expenditures, such as purchase charges, remodeling supplies, labor, permits, and contingencies. Break down the budget into particular areas, allowing for easier cost monitoring and analysis.

**Utilize Project Management Software:** Invest in project management software or budget monitoring solutions built exclusively for home flipping projects. These technologies expedite the process by categorizing spending, delivering real-time updates, and creating reports to track the budget's success.

***Keep detailed records:*** Maintain detailed records of all project-related spending, including receipts, invoices, and contracts. Organize these records logically, making it easier to evaluate and reconcile spending against the budget.

***Regularly Review and Adjust the Budget:*** Continuously check the budget's performance throughout the remodeling process. Compare actual expenses versus the projected amounts and discover any variances. Make required modifications to control spending efficiently and handle possible budget overruns swiftly.

***Prioritize Cost Control Measures:*** Implement cost-saving solutions without sacrificing quality. Seek competitive quotes from contractors, research bulk material discounts, and examine alternate suppliers to cut expenditures. Constantly analyze if particular design decisions or improvements match with the project's budgetary goals.

***Communicate and work together:*** Encourage open communication with the project team, which includes the designers, contractors, and suppliers. Communicate the needs of the budget and make sure that everyone is aware of their responsibilities regarding the budget that has been set. Regular meetings and reporting on progress help identify and manage potential financial challenges at an earlier stage.

***Plan for Contingencies:*** Set up a contingency reserve within the budget to accommodate for unexpected costs or unanticipated obstacles. Flipping a property typically contains surprises, such as hidden structural difficulties or permission delays, so having a cash buffer is vital for navigating these unanticipated events.

## DIY vs. Hiring Contractors: Pros and Cons

Factors to consider while considering whether to DIY or contract out chores. When it comes to flipping properties, determining whether to do it yourself (DIY) or hiring pros to take care of responsibilities may be a tough option. Here are some variables to consider:

Skill level

1. Evaluate own skills
2. Determine whether jobs require professional competence
3. Assessing your own skill level is vital to selecting which jobs to take on and which ones to employ specialists for. Certain operations, such as electrical work or plumbing, require specific knowledge and expertise that the typical individual may not have.

Time availability

- Assess how much time is required for each task
- Decide if time limits allow for DIY or need hiring

Another key issue when determining whether to DIY or pay professionals is the time required to finish each operation. If you have a tight timeframe and your personal schedule does not allow for much spare time, hiring pros may be the best alternative to ensuring the job is done on time.

Budget

- Weigh DIY expenses vs. professional charges
- Determine whether activities can be done within budget:One of the greatest elements to consider when flipping a property is the finances. Weighing the expenses of completing chores yourself vs. hiring specialists is vital to evaluating whether projects can be done within your budget. Keep in mind that sometimes employing specialists may actually save you money in the long run, as they are less likely to make errors that might wind up costing more to rectify. Ultimately, the choice of DIY or hiring specialists depends on your own circumstances and the exact activities that need to be accomplished. It is crucial to thoroughly examine the variables outlined above before making any judgments.

## *Pros and Cons of DIY*

House flipping may be a fun and successful business, but it requires a lot of hard work and decision-making. One of the important options is whether to undertake the job yourself or to employ professionals. There are benefits and downsides to both techniques, and it is necessary to analyze them thoroughly before making a choice.

## *Pros of DIY*

***Savings on labor expenses:*** When you perform the job yourself, you may save a substantial amount of money on labor costs.

***Personal pleasure and pride in work:*** There is something rewarding about performing the job yourself and seeing the rewards of your hard work.

***Learning and sharpening abilities:*** DIY projects are a terrific way to gain new skills and enhance your current ones.

## *Cons of DIY*

***Risks of probable errors and extra costs:*** If you make mistakes, it might wind up costing you more in the long run. And, in other situations, errors might result in significant safety hazards.

***Time-consuming:*** DIY projects may take a lot of time, which can be a difficulty if you have other commitments or if you want to complete the project fast.

When considering whether to manage a project yourself, it is vital to assess the possible rewards against the risks and downsides. Consider your skill level, the nature of the project, and the amount of time you have available. If you do decide to take on a project, make sure you have a strong strategy in place and that you have all the essential equipment and supplies.

## *Pros and Cons of Hiring Professionals*

### *Pros of Hiring Professionals*
***Quality work and experience:*** Hiring specialists guarantees that every activity in home flipping is done efficiently and with accuracy, owing to their knowledge and experience. They understand the ins and outs of property flipping, which makes their service more dependable.
***Saving time and decreasing stress:*** House flipping may be a difficult and time-consuming procedure. Hiring pros to complete the job may

save you time, enabling you to concentrate on other crucial parts of home flipping. It also decreases stress levels because you know that specialists are managing the critical responsibilities.

***Liability & insurance coverage:*** Professionals provide liability and insurance coverage in case of accidents or damage to your property. You are covered from any responsibility, which takes the load off you, guaranteeing that you have complete peace of mind.

## Cons of Hiring Professionals

***Costly labor costs:*** One of the primary downsides of employing specialists is that it may be fairly costly. Professionals demand a hefty fee for their services, which might cut into your earnings if you are not cautious.

***risk for misunderstanding and poor work:*** There is a risk for miscommunication and unsatisfactory work because you are not the one performing the task. You may have different views or procedures compared to the pros, which might lead to disagreements in vision or job outcomes.

It is crucial to analyze the advantages and downsides of hiring specialists thoroughly before opting to go down this road. If you are seeking excellent work and efficient outcomes, experts are the way to go. However, bear in mind that it might be fairly pricey.

## Hands-On or Help Wanted? Deciding What to Tackle Yourself During Your Remodel

The success of a property flip hinges on multiple factors, with renovation costs being a critical one. By adopting these key strategies for managing your renovation budget, you can ensure a smooth and efficient project that keeps you on track for a profitable outcome.

***Break down each task into individual Parts:*** Before determining which jobs to DIY or outsource, the first step is to break down each task into smaller sections. This will help you comprehend the difficulty of the work and the abilities necessary to perform it.

***Evaluate Each Part for Skill Requirements, Time Constraints, and Budget:*** Once you've broken down each activity, the next step is to examine each portion for skill needs, time restrictions, and money. This can help you assess if it's more cost-effective and time-efficient to do it yourself or employ a professional.

***A thorough inspection is the cornerstone for making informed decisions regarding your renovation project:*** By meticulously evaluating the property's condition, you can craft a strategic plan that leverages both your own skills and professional expertise. Tasks that fall within your comfort zone and capabilities, such as painting or basic landscaping, can be tackled as DIY projects. This allows you to save on labor costs and inject a touch of personalization into the renovation. However, for tasks that demand specialized knowledge or equipment, like electrical or plumbing work, delegating to qualified professionals is paramount. Their expertise ensures safety, adherence to building codes, and a higher quality of work, potentially saving you time and money in the long run by preventing costly mistakes.

***Consider Hiring a Contractor for Comprehensive House Flipping Management:*** If you are hesitant about handling all the duties alone, consider hiring a contractor for full home flipping management. A contractor may manage all parts of the project, including recruiting subcontractors, ensuring work is done to code, and managing the budget and deadline.

**List of Feasible DIY House Flipping Tasks**
• Painting
• Landscaping
• Installing Cabinets
• Installing flooring

- Replacing Fixtures
- Replacing Hardware

**Bringing in the Big Guns: When Flipping Requires Professional Expertise**
- Electrical Work
- Plumbing
- Roofing
- Structural Changes
- Foundation Problems
- Asbestos Removal

By examining each task and breaking them down into smaller sections, you can select which chores to DIY and which ones to outsource to specialists. Remember to consider time limits, talent needs, and money while making your selection. And if you're worried about managing the job yourself, consider hiring a professional for thorough home flipping management.

**Resources for DIY jobs:** House flipping entails numerous chores that need to be done, and sometimes it may be hard to determine whether to do them yourself or pay someone else to do them. But DIY chores may save you money and time. Here are some tools to help you manage DIY tasks:

**DIY tutorials and guides**

If you are new to DIY, then numerous tutorials and guidelines may help you master new skills and approaches. YouTube is a terrific place to start since you can find a lesson for practically anything, from repairing a broken faucet to tiling a bathroom. Other websites that provide DIY instructions include Pinterest, DIY Network, and Instructables.

***Home improvement stores:*** Home improvement shops are a fantastic resource for DIY jobs. Most have competent personnel who can give advice and help you find the correct equipment and supplies for your job. They also give seminars and workshops to educate people on DIY skills and methods. Home Depot, Lowe's, and

Menards are some of the leading home improvement retailers that provide these services.

***Online recommendations and reviews:*** Before you start any DIY project, it's crucial to do your homework and read reviews regarding equipment and supplies. You may locate reviews on home improvement websites such as Home Advisor, Houzz, and Angie's List. Social media channels like Facebook groups or Reddit forums are also fantastic locations to ask for tips and guidance from DIYers who have faced similar issues.

***Friends and relatives with skill or experience:*** Another resource for DIY jobs is friends and family members who have knowledge or experience. Chances are, someone in your network has the skills and experience you need to handle a given job. Reach out to them for guidance or aid, and they could even teach you new skills along the way. Do not hesitate to ask for assistance, since it might save you time and money. In brief, these materials may help you manage DIY projects and make the process smoother. With the correct equipment, supplies, and direction, you can execute DIY jobs with confidence and save money in the process.

## Level Up Your Flip: How to Recruit the Best Contractors for Every Job

Research and verify contractors' licenses, qualifications, and insurance
• Check with your state's contractor licensing board for rules and restrictions.
mitigate risk by verifying the contractor's license is current and in good standing.
• Ask for evidence of insurance, including liability and workers' compensation.
Check for prior job experience, outcomes, and references

- Ask for a portfolio of prior work and outcomes to evaluate whether the contractor is capable of finishing your job.
- Inquire for references and call them to inquire about their experience dealing with the contractor.
- Look for internet reviews and ratings to obtain a sense of the contractor's reputation.

Compare multiple specialists and their pricing

- Get quotations from various experts to compare pricing and services.
- Make sure the quotations include all required supplies, labor, and any additional charges.
- Beware of drastically low-priced estimates, since this may suggest a low-quality contractor or possible fraud.

Be careful of warning indications of frauds or low-quality professionals

- Avoid contractors that expect full payment beforehand or ask for cash-only payments.
- Beware of contractors that offer drastically cheaper pricing than others or who urge you to make a rapid decision. • Read contracts carefully and make sure they contain all important

facts, such as the project timetable, payment plan, and materials utilized.

Finding trustworthy specialists for your home flipping activities demands considerable study and cautious choices. Be careful to examine licenses, certificates, and insurance; check work experience, outcomes, and references; compare various pros; and be aware of warning indications of fraud or low-quality contractors.

# Selling the Deal: Marketingand Negotiation Strategies

The necessity of bargaining cannot be overemphasized in home flipping. A smart negotiator may get a home at a price that provides a considerable profit margin after remodeling expenditures and selling charges. It also offers you a chance to lessen the risks of the enterprise by negotiating advantageous contract terms with contractors and suppliers. The purpose of this book is to help you negotiate agreements efficiently in home flipping. We will review some techniques and methods that successful home flippers employ to acquire lucrative transactions. The chapter will also address some of the major pitfalls that you should avoid while negotiating a transaction.

***Preparation:*** Preparing for a negotiation for a home flip transaction is key. Taking the time to investigate and come up with a great offer may make all the difference. Proper preparation can make all the difference in the success of your house-flipping project. Here are some suggestions to get you started.

**Research the property and market thoroughly:** Look into the history of the home, including any faults or repairs that need to be done. Be mindful of the location, demographics of the region, and any impending projects that may affect the property value.

**Determine your target profit and budget:** Analyze the costs associated with the repairs and renovations you plan on doing to the house. Figure out how much profit you need to make and how much you are willing to spend on the property.

**Come up with an offer based on the property's valuation and your budget:** Make sure you give opportunity for discussion while still giving a reasonable price. Be prepared to defend your offer with market research and any required repairs.

***Consider your bargaining leverage:*** identify any important selling points you have, such as a rapid closing date or an all-cash offer. Use them to your advantage during negotiations.

***Anticipate probable objections or issues:*** Come up with answers ahead of time to any concerns the seller may have. Addressing these concerns upfront tells the seller that you are serious and prepared.

***Forge a Positive Connection:*** More than just a transaction, house flipping thrives on building a connection with the seller. By actively listening to their concerns and demonstrating courtesy throughout the process, you can create a more collaborative environment. This fosters trust and understanding, ultimately leading to smoother negotiations and a higher chance of a successful sale for everyone involved.

In the fast-paced world of house flipping, meticulous preparation is your secret weapon for negotiation: Thorough research on the property and local market should inform your offer, which should be both strong in value and realistic within your budget. Anticipating potential objections and crafting persuasive responses demonstrates your seriousness and preparedness. Building a rapport with the seller fosters a more collaborative atmosphere, ultimately increasing your chances of securing a favorable outcome.

***Communication:*** Effective communication is an essential aspect of any negotiation, including house flipping deals. Good communication skills can help you build a positive rapport with the seller and the real estate agent, convey your ideas effectively, and better understand the other party's needs and requirements.

## *importance of effective communication in negotiation*

The Power of Communication: Effective communication is the cornerstone of successful negotiation in house flipping. It unlocks a two-pronged advantage:

**Building Rapport:** By fostering open communication with the seller and the real estate agent, you can build trust and establish a strong connection. This collaborative environment allows for a more pleasant negotiation process.

**Understanding Needs:** Effective communication goes beyond just talking. By actively listening to their responses and asking insightful questions, you gain a valuable understanding of the seller's needs, wants, and expectations. This knowledge empowers you to craft a more compelling offer and navigate negotiations with greater finesse.

**Clearly Articulate Your Value:** Effective communication isn't a one-way street. You also need to be able to transmit your ideas, opinions, and recommendations clearly and concisely. This is especially crucial when presenting your offer.

## Mastering the Art of Negotiation: Communication Strategies for Success

Negotiating a house flip hinges on effective communication. Here are key strategies to build rapport and navigate discussions with confidence:

***Be respectful and approachable:*** Professional courtesy is paramount. Maintain a pleasant tone, actively listen, and avoid interrupting. This fosters a collaborative environment conducive to finding common ground.

***Ask insightful questions:*** Curiosity is your friend. Open-ended questions like "What's your ideal timeline for closing?" or "Are there any specific concerns you have about the process?" demonstrate your attentiveness and gather valuable information to tailor your approach.

***Become an active listener:*** Communication is a two-way street. Pay close attention to the seller's and agent's responses. Try to see things from their perspective. This understanding empowers you to address their needs and craft mutually beneficial solutions.

*Address concerns proactively:* Do not shy away from objections. Acknowledge them directly and work collaboratively to find solutions that satisfy everyone involved. This demonstrates your professionalism and commitment to a smooth transaction.

## Crafting a Winning Offer: Make a Strong First Impression

Presenting a compelling offer is a critical step in securing a successful house flip. Here's how to make yours stand out:

*Be Ready to Strike:* Preparation is key. Ensure you have all the necessary documentation readily available, including your offer letter, pre-approval letter, and proof of funds. This demonstrates professionalism and seriousness toward the seller.

***Focus on the value proposition:*** Highlight the benefits for the seller. Do you offer a quick closing timeline? Flexibility on closing dates? A smooth and transparent process? Emphasize how your offer solves their needs and streamlines the transaction.

***Embrace Collaboration:*** Negotiation is a dance. Be prepared to find common ground. Demonstrate a willingness to compromise on certain aspects while confidently advocating for your key interests.

***End on a Positive Note:*** Leave a lasting impression. Regardless of the outcome, conclude the negotiation on a courteous and professional note. This fosters a positive relationship with the seller and agent, which could prove beneficial in future endeavors.

***Flexibility:*** Negotiating deals in house flipping requires a lot of skill, patience, and flexibility. Being flexible during negotiations is crucial because it helps you navigate unexpected obstacles that may arise during the negotiation process.

## The Importance of Flexibility in Negotiation

1. Flexibility is key to a successful negotiation. It allows you to adapt to changing circumstances, make the most of unexpected opportunities, and navigate unforeseen obstacles.

2. Being flexible also helps you maintain control of the negotiation. It allows you to adjust your strategy based on new information or developments, ensuring that you stay one step ahead of the other party.

3. Moreover, flexibility demonstrates your willingness to work with the seller to find a mutually beneficial solution. It shows that you are open to compromise and willing to listen to the seller's concerns.

## Overcoming Hurdles and Finding Common Ground: The Negotiation Dance

Negotiations rarely follow a perfectly straight path. Unexpected obstacles can arise, testing your composure and adaptability. Here's how to navigate these situations:

***Stay Calm and collected:*** Keep your cool. Do not get discouraged or walk away prematurely. Instead, take a deep breath and focus on solutions.

***Collaborative Problem-Solving:*** Work together. Identify the root cause of the issue and explore creative solutions with the seller. Brainstorm possibilities and be open to adjusting your expectations if necessary. For example, if the price is a sticking point, consider offering a quicker closing or covering some closing costs in exchange for a more favorable purchase price.

***Understanding the Seller's Needs:*** See things from their perspective. Ask thoughtful questions and actively listen to their concerns. Finding common ground is key. Perhaps you both share a desire for a fast closure or to minimize disruption to their lives.

***Building Rapport:*** Connect on a human level. Look for opportunities to establish rapport. Do you share any common interests or goals? Discuss your vision for the property and how it aligns with their plans. Building a positive connection can foster a more collaborative negotiation environment.

Remember, negotiation is a two-way street. Flexibility is crucial. By adapting to changing circumstances, addressing unexpected hurdles, and finding common ground with the seller, you'll be well-positioned to secure a win-win outcome for everyone involved. Negotiation is a process, so maintain patience, stay focused, and be prepared to work together toward a mutually beneficial solution.

# Closing the Deal: Sealing the Flip and Securing Your Investment

The closing process is the momentous culmination, where all the meticulous planning, extensive negotiations, and calculated risks come to fruition. A successful closing signifies the official transfer of ownership from the seller to you, marking the official start of your renovation phase. Because of this immense importance, proper execution of the closing process is paramount. Here is a comprehensive guide to navigating this crucial step:

### *The Importance of Closing*

***The Final Handshake:*** Think of closing as the official handshake in a business deal. During this stage, you'll finalize all the agreed-upon terms, meticulously review and sign the contract, and formally take ownership of the property. This legally binding agreement grants you full rights and responsibilities associated with the property.

Without a successful closing, your investment efforts stall. Remember, thorough preparation is key to avoiding any unforeseen obstacles that could jeopardize the entire process.

*Addressing Last-Minute Concerns:* Finding Common Ground: It's not uncommon for sellers to raise final objections, even after reaching a tentative agreement. These concerns could arise due to various reasons, such as unexpected personal circumstances or a lingering uncertainty about a specific detail in the contract. The key here is to listen attentively to their apprehensions and strive for solutions that benefit everyone involved. Be prepared to revisit certain negotiation points and find compromises that create a mutually agreeable outcome. Focus on understanding the root of their hesitations and offering alternative solutions that effectively address their needs. Patience, empathy, and a willingness to find common ground are crucial during this stage.

*Post-Closing Procedures:* Securing Your Investment: Once the deal is officially sealed and the contract is signed, take immediate steps to secure your investment. Obtain the keys to the property from the seller, change the locks to ensure your control, and secure the premises as soon as possible. This could involve setting up a security system or boarding up any vacant entry points. Furthermore, ensure you have all relevant documents readily available, such as the mortgage agreement, the deed transferring ownership to you, and the title insurance policy that protects you against any unforeseen ownership claims. Having these documents organized and accessible will be crucial throughout the renovation and resale process. Now that you've successfully navigated the closing process, you can begin the exciting renovation phase, transforming the property according to your vision!

***Patience is Key:*** Anticipating and Managing Delays: Expect delays during the closing process. Financing approvals, inspections, or appraisals can sometimes take longer than anticipated, causing setbacks in the timeline.

Stay patient and focused on the end goal. Maintain open communication with all parties involved, such as the seller, your lender, and any relevant inspectors. By proactively addressing any concerns that emerge promptly, you can minimize the impact of delays and keep the process moving forward.

***Avoid Rushing the Process:*** Prioritizing Careful Review: One of the biggest closing mistakes investors make is rushing through the process. Remember, haste can lead to costly and avoidable errors. Take the time to thoroughly review all documentation involved in the closing process, including the final contract, loan documents, and title reports. Ensure that every detail aligns with the previously agreed-upon terms and that there are no discrepancies. Don't hesitate to ask clarifying questions if anything seems unclear. By prioritizing careful review, you can safeguard your investment and avoid any potential complications down the road.

## Crafting a Compelling Marketing Strategy: Attract Your Ideal Buyer

A successful house flip hinges not only on a smart purchase and renovation but also on a well-executed marketing campaign. Whether you choose to go the DIY route or partner with a real estate agent, the ultimate goal remains the same: selling your property quickly and for the best possible price.

Reaching the Right Audience: To achieve this goal, attracting a wide range of qualified buyers is crucial. Here is a two-pronged approach to consider:

*Understanding Buyer Behavior:* Identify where potential buyers typically search for properties. Popular online real estate platforms like Realtor.com, Zillow, and Trulia offer comprehensive listings categorized by location. The majority of these listings are uploaded by real estate agents through the Multiple Listing Service (MLS). Many newspapers also subscribe to the MLS, feeding fresh listings to their online platforms, making these websites essential tools for real estate marketing.

***Targeted Marketing:*** While online exposure is important, consider targeted marketing efforts to reach buyers most likely to be interested in your specific property. For instance, if you've flipped a charming log cabin nestled in the woods, acquiring a mailing list from a local outdoor equipment store and sending targeted direct mail or email blasts could be highly effective.

Effective Marketing Channels: The real estate marketing landscape offers a diverse mix of online and offline channels to reach potential buyers:

***Online Advertising:*** Leverage the power of the internet. Explore free advertising options on websites like vFlyer, Point2, and Postlets. These platforms may also syndicate your listing to other high-traffic websites, maximizing your reach.

***Direct Mail (Targeted):*** While print advertising like newspapers and magazines may have waned in effectiveness, strategically targeted direct mail campaigns can still yield results. By acquiring mailing lists from businesses or organizations whose clientele aligns with your ideal buyer profile, you can send targeted mailers or email blasts that resonate with their interests.

***Offline Strategies:*** Do not underestimate the power of traditional methods. A well-placed "For Sale" sign in a prominent location on your property can spark inquiries from passersby. If your property has limited street visibility, explore the possibility of partnering with a neighbor to display a directional sign on their property. Remember, a polite request can go a long way.

By implementing a strategic marketing plan that combines online exposure, targeted outreach, and well-placed signage, you can effectively attract a pool of qualified buyers eager to see your beautifully transformed property, increasing your chances of a successful and profitable house flip.

## What should your marketing convey?

Transforming the sale of your house from a practical need to an enticing opportunity hinges on the power of effective advertising. While crafting house ad copy might seem like an artistic endeavor, there are proven strategies that ensure your message resonates with your target audience. The key lies in striking a delicate balance: emphasize the positive features of your property without veering into unsubstantiated claims. Facts and figures are crucial, but avoid unverified details like square footage that could raise red flags later. Instead, paint a picture with evocative language. Focus on subjective descriptions like "spacious," "expansive," or "abundant" to convey a sense of a comfortable living area.

Beyond dimensions, capture the essence of the home. Weave words that evoke emotions and imagery, allowing potential buyers to envision themselves inhabiting the space. Describe the architectural style, is it a charming craftsman bungalow or a modern masterpiece? Highlight the layout and flow—does the open floor plan create a sense of togetherness, or do cozy nooks offer inviting retreats? Do not forget the amenities! Mention the sparkling pool, the gourmet kitchen, or the finished basement—features that elevate a house into a dream home. Remember, location is king! Proximity to desirable amenities plays a significant role in a buying decision. Mention the house's idyllic location nestled between two parks, its convenient access to shopping centers, or its closeness to top-rated schools. Craft a title that goes beyond the generic "House for Sale." Think about what makes your property unique—a sprawling backyard perfect for family gatherings and a sun-drenched balcony overlooking a vibrant cityscape. Leverage those unique features in the title to pique interest.

Finally, infuse your ad copy with positive language. Instead of simply stating facts, weave words that create a positive emotional connection. Describe the home as "charming," "delightful," or "inviting," or for a secluded haven, "peaceful" or "tranquil." By following these guidelines and showcasing your property's true potential, you'll be well on your way to attracting serious buyers and achieving a successful sale

## Sale By Owner Vs. Realtor

Thinking about going the For-Sale-by-Owner (FSBO) route to pocket the realtor commission? While FSBO can be a tempting cost-saving strategy, it's essential to understand the significant time investment and specific skillset required to navigate the process successfully.

Before deciding to tackle FSBO, take stock of the following key responsibilities that will fall squarely on your shoulders:

***Market Savvy:*** In-depth research is crucial. You'll need to become an expert on comparable properties in your area, analyze recent sales data, and understand current market trends. This knowledge is essential to setting a competitive listing price that attracts buyers without leaving money on the table.

***Marketing Mastermind:*** Presentation is key in today's real estate market. Craft compelling descriptions that showcase your property's unique selling points. Invest in high-quality photography, capturing both the home's interior and exterior in the best possible light. Don't underestimate the power of visuals; professional photos can significantly increase buyer interest. Additionally, strategically list your property on relevant real estate websites with wide exposure to potential buyers.

***Legal Liaisons:*** The legal side of selling a home can be complex. Ensure you obtain and complete all necessary legal disclosures to avoid potential delays or complications during the sales process.

Understanding your legal obligations will protect you and ensure a smooth transaction.

***Showtime Superstar:*** Selling your home often involves multiple showings and open houses. Be prepared to maintain flexible availability to accommodate potential buyers' schedules. This might require adjustments to your routine and a commitment to keeping your home presentable for viewings.

***Negotiation Ninja:*** Offers can come with complexities. You'll need to be able to evaluate offers carefully, understand contingencies like inspections and appraisals, and effectively negotiate terms to secure the best possible outcome for yourself. Honing your negotiation skills can make a significant difference in your final sale price.

FSBO (for sale by owner) can offer a sense of accomplishment and potentially some cost savings. However, it's crucial to realistically assess your time commitment, market knowledge, and negotiation skills. Busy professionals or those unfamiliar with the real estate landscape might find the FSBO process overwhelming. A qualified real estate agent can streamline the process, providing valuable expertise in market analysis, marketing strategy, legal compliance, and negotiation. Many sellers underestimate the intricate role agents play in navigating the complexities of selling a home until they experience the demands of FSBO firsthand.

**Staging to Sell: The Secret Weapon for Faster Sales**

Do not let your property languish on the market! Staging is a proven strategy that goes beyond mere curb appeal. It's about creating an emotional connection with potential buyers, allowing them to envision themselves living in your space and experiencing the lifestyle it offers. An empty house leaves too much to the imagination. Staging bridges that gap, showcasing the functionality, potential, and emotional appeal of your property.

## Unlocking the Power of Staging:

***Boost Curb Appeal:*** First impressions matter! Power wash your exterior to remove grime and make it sparkle. Plant flowers, add colorful accents with potted plants or a brightly painted door, and create an inviting entranceway. This sets the tone for a well-maintained home.

***Maximize Space Perception:*** Declutter ruthlessly! Counter tops, cupboards, drawers, and closets should all appear spacious and organized. Overcrowded spaces make the house feel smaller. Potential buyers need to be able to imagine their own furniture and belongings fitting comfortably.

***Showcase Functionality:*** Stage furniture arrangements that demonstrate how a room can be used. A dining table set for a meal with attractive place settings, strategically placed furniture in the living room that creates conversation areas—all paint a picture of comfortable living. Don't forget smaller spaces like bathrooms! Stage towels neatly and add decorative touches to convey a spa-like feel.

*Neutral Palette:* Opt for neutral color schemes that create a sense of calm and allow buyers to imagine their own décor. Bold colors or patterned wallpaper can be alienating to some tastes.

*Highlight Key Areas:* Master bedrooms should exude luxury. Stage the bed with high-quality linens and add inviting throw pillows. Show off the versatility of additional rooms by staging them as offices, gyms, or play areas. Find creative uses for nooks and alcoves, perhaps with a cozy reading chair or a small home office setup.

*Fresh and Inviting Ambiance:* Ensure a pleasant scent throughout the house. Avoid artificial air fresheners and opt for natural solutions like fresh flowers or baking cookies before a show. A clean and fresh smell creates a positive first impression.

## Considering professional help?

Many home flippers lack the furniture inventory for proper staging, or their properties might have unique layouts that can be challenging for buyers to visualize. This is where professional stagers come in. Their expertise is especially valuable for unique properties or those that need a little extra TLC to reach their full sales potential.

***Staging Costs:*** Staging is typically priced with an initial fixed fee followed by a monthly rental fee. Costs vary depending on your location, the size of your property, and the scope of the staging project. Expect to invest at least a few thousand dollars, but view it as an investment that can significantly increase your return by selling your property faster and potentially for a higher price.

***Focus on key rooms:*** Not every room needs professional staging. However, prioritize rooms with unique layouts or unclear functionality.

Master bedrooms, living rooms, and dining areas should be staged for maximum impact. For smaller homes, consider strategically staging a few key rooms to showcase the property's potential.

## Capture Attention and Boost Value: Essential DIY Home Staging Tips

*Emphasize Improvements:* Draw viewers' eyes to the renovations and upgrades you have implemented. This initial visual impact can significantly influence their overall impression of the property.

*Timeless Appeal with Neutral Accents:* Create a welcoming and spacious atmosphere by utilizing a neutral color palette. Introduce pops of color and decorative elements sparingly to avoid overwhelming potential buyers.

***Staged for Success:*** Ensure your home is consistently presentable and clutter-free for impromptu buyer showings. This meticulous presentation demonstrates pride of ownership and sets the stage for a positive buying experience.

***Strategic Enhancements:*** To elevate specific areas without breaking the bank, explore the option of borrowing or renting high-quality furniture. Similarly, consider budget-friendly bathroom upgrades like new towels, shower curtains, and decorative curtains. These minor improvements can yield a significant return on investment by creating a more polished and inviting space.

## Transforming Your Open House into a Buyer Magnet

**For properties with a real estate agent:**

1. Establish a clear understanding with your agent regarding the property's most attractive

features. Collaborate on crafting a compelling narrative that showcases these strengths during the open house.

2. Before the agent arrives, ensure the space is meticulously prepared. This includes a thorough cleaning, refreshing the yard with mowing and landscaping, and clearing any snow accumulation (depending on your location). A sparkling first impression is essential.

### For FSBO (For Sale By Owner) properties:

1. Leverage the power of online real estate platforms to maximize exposure to potential buyers actively searching for homes in your area.

2. Don't underestimate the impact of local advertising. Eye-catching signage in the neighborhood can pique the curiosity of passersby who might be interested.

3. Go beyond standard marketing channels. Consider targeted outreach through social groups, schools, and religious institutions frequented by your ideal buyer demographic. This allows you to connect with potential buyers who may not be actively searching online but are receptive to opportunities within their community.

## The Art of Hosting

Regardless of whether you have an agent:

***Become a Temporary Agent:*** Step into the role of a knowledgeable and welcoming host. Be prepared to answer questions about the property's features and neighborhood amenities.

***Highlight, Do Not Hover:*** Direct attention to the property's most compelling aspects during the open house. This could involve showcasing recent renovations, unique architectural details, or the functionality of the floor plan. However, avoid following potential buyers around the house. Instead, maintain a presence that allows them to explore the space at their own pace while remaining readily available to address any questions they may have.

***Strike a balance:*** While it's important to be approachable and informative, avoid being overly solicitous. Potential buyers appreciate having space to envision themselves living in the home. Your attentiveness should demonstrate that you're a helpful resource but not create a feeling of being pressured.

## The Art of the Wait: Cultivating Patience for a Successful Sale

***Trusting the Process:*** Patience is a Virtue Following the right strategies takes time to yield results. If you have implemented essential steps like market-driven adjustments, a compelling presentation through effective marketing and staging, and strategic pricing guided by market data and professional advice, then a little patience is crucial. While it's understandable to desire a quick sale, a rushed approach could lead to missed opportunities.

## Gauging Interest and Refining Your Strategy: Insights Lead to Action

***Prime Time:*** Allow a few weeks after launching your marketing campaign for showings to materialize. This ensures ample time for potential buyers to discover your listing through online platforms, yard signs, or community outreach. Don't be discouraged by a lack of immediate offers. A steady stream of showings is a positive indicator.

***Agent Insights:*** Regularly communicate with your agent. They are a valuable resource who can provide feedback from potential buyers who viewed your property but didn't make an offer. This feedback can be a gold mine of information. Listen carefully to understand their concerns and identify areas for improvement to strengthen your position in the market.

***Addressing Concerns:*** If there are minor repairs or cosmetic updates identified through buyer feedback or your assessment, consider them. Addressing these issues demonstrates attentiveness to detail and a commitment to providing a move-in-ready space. This can improve buyer confidence and eliminate potential roadblocks to a sale.

## Creative Solutions and Flexibility: Adapting to Market Dynamics

***Tailored Incentives:*** Be open to offering creative incentives that resonate with your target buyers and address their current needs. For example, if oil prices are a concern in your area, offering a full tank of oil to the new homeowner demonstrates understanding and can sweeten the deal, making your property a more attractive option.

***Realistic Expectations:*** Maintaining realistic expectations about the selling timeframe is essential. While a well-priced and well-presented home will attract interest, market conditions can influence the pace of offers. Understanding this dynamic allows you to adjust your strategy if needed, without succumbing to discouragement.

***Patience, Adaptability, and Results:*** By combining patience with a willingness to adapt and address buyer concerns, you can increase your chances of a successful sale. Remember, a thoughtful and strategic approach can turn waiting time into a period of productive fine-tuning for a smoother sales experience. Be prepared to make adjustments based on market feedback and embrace creative solutions. This

A proactive approach will position you to achieve your real estate goals.

## Pricing Strategies for Maximum Profit

You have developed the perfect product or service that your customers will adore. Your landing page is prepped, and your marketing ideas are bursting with potential. But hold on before unleashing this masterpiece on the world. There's a crucial step you cannot skip: nailing the perfect price. It is a balancing act. Charge too much, and you scare away buyers; go too low, and your profits disappear. The key is finding the sweet spot—a price that benefits both you and your target audience. That's where pricing strategies come in.

## Your Pricing Strategy: The Secret Weapon

Think of your pricing strategy as a secret weapon for setting the ideal price. It meticulously considers everything that impacts your profit margin, both internal (production costs) and external (competitor pricing, market trends). This data-driven approach eliminates guesswork and ensures your pricing decisions are logical, not based on intuition. A well-defined pricing strategy also forces you to delve into market research, stripping away any personal biases you might have about your product's "worth."

## Unlocking Maximum Sales Potential: A Toolkit of Pricing Strategies

The world of pricing is not a one-size-fits-all scenario. Businesses have a toolbox of pricing strategies at their disposal, each with unique strengths and ideal uses. A Look at Popular Pricing Schemes. Your organization does not have to adopt one form of pricing approach exclusively. To best accomplish your company objectives, you may always mix and match various pricing methods with different goods or services. (You can see this in action with Tesla, which offers Model S vehicles at a premium price and Model 3 cars for half the cost.) You may also vary your approach if your sales objectives, manufacturing costs, and outcomes change.

As you start developing the appropriate balance of pricing techniques for your purposes, consider these eight possibilities and their distinct benefits:

**Cost-plus pricing:** Cost-plus pricing is one of the simplest and most popular pricing techniques that firms adopt. With this strategy, just add a percent-based markup to your product cost, and you'll know what to charge. For example, if the wholesale price of a sofa is $500 and a furniture business wants to sell it at a 50% markup, they might apply the calculation (500 × 0.5) + 500 to arrive at their final retail price: $750. Keystone pricing, which always doubles the product cost, is a particularly popular subset of this method. Cost-plus pricing is a simple approach for merchants—particularly those with huge inventory like grocery shops—to "modernize retail pricing through automation and simplification strategies." (This underlines the improvement in efficiency.) It also assures a profit margin that you are pleased with on every transaction. However, this technique doesn't do a great job at taking into account labor or external issues like competition. It's not the ideal solution for firms that offer digital items or services, either.

***Value pricing:*** Value pricing revolutionizes the traditional cost-centric approach to pricing strategy. Instead of simply covering production expenses, it compels businesses to adopt a customer-centric perspective. This shift in focus prioritizes the perceived worth a customer assigns to a product or service. It's no longer just about the tangible features; value pricing demands a deeper understanding of the less quantifiable aspects that shape a customer's perception of value. Economic conditions, for example, can significantly influence how much a customer believes something is worth. During a recession, businesses that price solely on production costs might struggle to maintain demand in a cost-conscious market. Value pricing, however, empowers businesses to adapt by adjusting pricing strategies to reflect the customer's perceived value during economic downturns.

Furthermore, value pricing fosters a dynamic relationship between a brand and its customers. A brand built on a strong reputation for quality, exceptional customer service, and a commitment to innovation commands a higher perceived value. This allows businesses to establish premium pricing strategies that resonate with their target audience. Conversely, negative publicity or a decline in product quality can erode trust and necessitate price reductions to maintain customer loyalty. Value pricing, therefore, incentivizes businesses to constantly innovate and refine their product offerings. Introducing features that enhance functionality, improve user experience, or address customer pain points can significantly increase perceived value. This opens doors to potentially justifying price increases or attracting new customer segments.

Imagine a company selling athletic wear. Traditionally, their pricing strategy might fluctuate significantly based on seasonal demand peaks. Value pricing, however, encourages a more holistic approach. By understanding the customer's perspective, the company can devise strategies that maintain customer interest year-round. This could involve highlighting the versatility of their athletic wear for various activities throughout the year, or launching targeted marketing campaigns focused on off-season activities like yoga or fitness training.

In essence, value pricing is a recipe for long-term success. By prioritizing customer satisfaction and aligning pricing strategy with perceived value, businesses can foster long-term customer loyalty and build a sustainable business model. It's a dynamic approach that empowers businesses to move beyond simply covering production costs; it's a strategy that lays the foundation for long-term success by building trust and customer loyalty through a pricing strategy that reflects the true value proposition.

***Penetration price:*** Penetration pricing starts with low prices to grab customers, then slowly raises prices as the business gets more popular. This helps you debut with a large number of sales right away. Penetration pricing may be particularly successful for startups and small firms that are still focusing on developing their brands. Though it may undoubtedly be hazardous, it's a terrific technique for you to attract buyers who may otherwise dismiss your goods or services. As you build brand recognition, trust, and a stable client base, you may switch to various pricing tactics that generate a bigger profit. It is crucial to recognize that penetration pricing varies from loss leader pricing, which is prohibited in many jurisdictions. Whereas penetration pricing swiftly raises your prices, a loss leader approach consistently employs low price points or promotions to acquire consumers, sometimes in hopes of forcing rivals out of business. This may lead to a monopoly, enabling the corporation to implement prices and gradually drop prices over time.

*Price skimming:* Price scheing is an efficient strategy to attract trendsetters and influencers who want to be the first to sample new goods and services. Doing so may make customers eager for items, while making high-income users devoted members of your client base.
This occurs routinely in the world of cellphones. When new iPhone models initially arrive, they may cost about $1,000 since they are incredibly fashionable. Over time, they grow more affordable for the majority, reaching individuals of diverse economic levels.

Another plus of price skimming is that you'll more rapidly recoup your manufacturing expenses instead of sustaining an early loss.

Price skimming does not work as effectively for organizations delivering professional services, such as accounting firms and business consultants, as they're not as substantially demand-driven. Subscription-based firms like meal kit services and SaaS brands may also have a hard time utilizing this technique, as high initial pricing does not motivate consumers to make long-term recurring payments.

However, price skimming may work successfully in businesses that depend on trends, like technology and fashion, or ones with extremely high manufacturing costs, such as medicines.

***Bundle price:*** Using a bundle pricing technique involves offering clients two or more items or services for a lesser cost than if they were to purchase them individually. For example, if an internet company offers dog food for $20 and a dog food dish for $10, they may offer both for $25 instead of $30.

Whether you're combining hotel rooms, flights, and car rentals like Expedia or bundling haircuts and styling like your favorite salon, this is a smart pricing approach that makes clients feel like they're receiving more for what they're spending. With bundles, your consumers are likely to spend more each time they come.

*Premium price:* In the dynamic world of business, crafting a pricing strategy that resonates with your target audience is paramount. For brands fortunate enough to cater to a clientele with a penchant for luxury, a captivating approach known as premium pricing emerges as a powerful tool. This strategy transcends the realm of simply maximizing profit margins; it's a meticulously crafted move designed to cultivate a brand image synonymous with exclusivity and desirability.

At its core, premium pricing hinges on intentionally setting prices higher than competitors. This creates a distinct separation from the pack, positioning your brand as a symbol of luxury. The act of commanding a premium price imbues your offerings with an aura of prestige, subtly communicating to consumers that they are acquiring not just a product or service, but a piece of something exceptional. Imagine a world of high-end fashion houses. Their garments are meticulously crafted using premium materials and boast impeccable design, justifying their significantly higher price points compared to mass-produced clothing. Similarly, think about luxury car brands. Their vehicles are not merely modes of transportation; they are symbols of status and success, a perception reinforced by the premium price tag.

The success of this strategy hinges on a deep understanding of your target audience. Premium pricing works best when you have a clear picture of your ideal customer— someone who appreciates and aspires to quality, exclusivity, and the status associated with luxury brands. For these discerning consumers, the higher price point becomes a badge of honor, a symbol of their discerning taste and ability to acquire the very best. Consider the example of high-end electronics. While basic models offer core functionality, premium brands command a higher price by incorporating cutting-edge technology, superior materials, and a sleek, sophisticated design aesthetic. These elements elevate the product from a functional device to a coveted status symbol.

However, it's crucial to remember that premium pricing is a double-edged sword. If your ideal customer is highly cost-conscious and prioritizes affordability, a premium price tag might alienate them. The key lies in ensuring your brand narrative, product quality, and overall customer experience consistently reinforce the value proposition that justifies the higher price. When executed flawlessly, premium pricing can be a powerful tool, propelling your brand to the forefront of the luxury market and fostering a loyal customer base willing to pay a premium for the exclusivity and exceptional quality your brand represents.

***Competitive price:*** If you are largely targeting price-sensitive clients, you may want to pursue a competitive pricing approach instead. With this method, you will keep prices lower than your rivals' prices. Brands like Best Buy and Target provide price match promises to maintain their loyal consumers, even when competing retailers have specials.

This technique is commonly linked with economy pricing, in which corporations concentrate on keeping manufacturing costs low to give the best price available.

While it will not make your business seem special in any way, competitive price can help you win over clients who are seeking a dependably reasonable product.

***Psychological pricing:*** While a couple of the approaches outlined may have a large influence on the perceived worth of your product or service, psychological pricing modifies the perceived price. It utilizes the following strategies to make clients feel like they're saving more or spending less than they actually are:

• Offering pricing slightly below a full number ($9.99 instead of $10) • Placing an initial price adjacent to a reduced price
• Launching a BOGO (buy one, get one free) deal that spotlights a free item instead of a 50% off discount

The most notable advantage of this strategy is that you can effectively establish the rates you desire while still keeping clients pleased. You may be able to entice a frugal consumer to spend more than usual, as they'll feel like they are getting a good deal. .

## Negotiation Tips for Closing the Deal

Negotiation is a critical component of finishing a real estate purchase effectively. Here are some guidelines to help you negotiate the negotiation process effectively:

**Do Your Homework:**
1. Research the property extensively, including its characteristics, condition, and previous sales in the neighborhood.

2. Understand current market circumstances, such as inventory levels, average days on market, and price trends.

3. Analyze comparable properties (comps) to determine the property's fair market worth and appraise its strengths and flaws compared to other listings.

*Establish Your Priorities*
1. Identify your must-have parameters, such as price, closing timeframe, or contingencies.
2. Determine your desired objective and the compromises you're prepared to make to attain it.
3. Prioritize your goals to guide your negotiating technique and decision-making process.

### Be Prepared to Walk Away
1. Define your bottom line or maximum threshold for the deal's terms and circumstances.
2. Have other ideas or backup plans in case discussions break down.
3. Demonstrate confidence and boldness by proving that you're prepared to walk away from a transaction that doesn't satisfy your standards.

### Build Rapport
1. Establish a good connection with the other person via open communication, respect, and empathy.
2. Listen carefully to their issues and perspectives to exhibit understanding and create trust.
3. Maintain professionalism and kindness throughout the negotiating process to create goodwill and collaboration.

### Listen Actively

1. Pay great attention to the other party's verbal and nonverbal signs to grasp their motives and interests.
2. Ask clarifying questions to acquire deeper insights into their requirements, preferences, and limits.
3. Reflect on their worries and respect their viewpoint to demonstrate empathy and develop connection.

**Focus on Win-Win Solutions:**
1. Look for mutually beneficial results that meet the interests and goals of both parties.
2. Brainstorm new ideas or compromises that fulfill each party's major goals.
3. Avoid adopting a zero-sum attitude when one party's benefit comes at the price of the other.

**Maintain Flexibility**
1. Remain open to altering your bargaining stance or making compromises to achieve a mutually acceptable agreement.
2. Seek common ground and seek other ideas to resolve impasses or conflicts.

3. Adapt your strategy depending on fresh knowledge or changing situations during negotiations.

**Stay calm and confident:**
1. Keep your emotions under control and keep a calm and confident manner during talks.
2. Project confidence in your opinions and suggestions to communicate credibility and influence.
3. Avoid responding quickly or emotionally to counteroffers or challenges during negotiations.

**Use stillness to your Advantage:**
1. Embrace times of stillness as opportunity to contemplate, organize your ideas, and urge the other side to react or make compromises.

2. Resist the impulse to fill the quiet with unneeded talk or compromises, since it might harm your negotiation stance.

## Document Everything
1. Record all negotiating talks, offers, and counteroffers in writing to produce a clear and thorough record of the negotiation process.
2. Document agreed-upon terms and conditions to avoid misunderstandings or disagreements after the fact.
3. Ensure that all parties participating in the discussion have access to the same information and documents.

## Seek Professional Advice
1. Consult with experienced professionals, such as real estate agents, lawyers, or negotiating specialists, for assistance and support.

2. Leverage their knowledge to handle complicated negotiating circumstances, grasp legal ramifications, and defend your interests successfully.

3. Consider outsourcing specific portions of the negotiating process to specialists who can advocate on your behalf and maximize results.

# Valuing Your Investment: Methods of Valuation

In today's dynamic real estate market, where the property flipping sector is developing rapidly, investors must grasp the subtleties of valuing these profitable projects. The property flipping sector in the US was valued at an astonishing $9.6 billion in 2020, and according to 2023 data, flip transactions accounted for approximately 8% of single-family- houses in the USA, boasting an average gross profit of 27.5%. Forecasts for 2024 anticipate a 5% nationwide growth in property prices, further reinforcing the attraction of house flipping. Capturing the appropriate chances may lead to big earnings. This chapter will lead you through crucial aspects and valuation methodologies that are vital for determining the viability of a property flipping company. From acquiring a complete grasp of the real estate market and trends to applying valuation methodologies such as the Comparable Sales Method and Income Approach,. The purpose of this chapter is to empower you with the information and skills to make informed choices. Let's delve deeper and identify the important aspects that lead to the success of properly flipping endeavors

## Understanding Different Valuation Methods

### *Comparable Methods*

In the fast-paced world of property flipping, where quick decisions and accurate valuations are paramount, the comparable sales approach emerges as an indispensable tool. This cornerstone technique empowers real estate investors and flippers to navigate the ever-changing market with confidence, transforming a potentially risky venture into a lucrative opportunity.

The essence of the comparable sales approach lies in leveraging the power of market data. By meticulously researching recent sales of similar properties in the surrounding area, flippers gain valuable insights into current market trends and pricing. These "comparable properties" serve as a benchmark, offering a realistic perspective on the potential value of the subject property after renovations are complete. Flippers embark on a rigorous analysis, meticulously scrutinizing factors such as size, condition, features, location, and most importantly, selling prices. The objective is to identify properties with the highest degree of similarity to the one being appraised.

Once a selection of comparable properties is identified, adjustments are made to their sale prices to account for any discrepancies with the subject property. These adjustments act as a fine-tuning mechanism, reflecting the relative value of various features. For example, a comparable property boasting an extra bedroom and a modern kitchen renovation might necessitate an upward adjustment to its sales price, while a property in need of significant repairs and lacking desirable amenities might warrant a downward adjustment. Common factors considered when making adjustments include:

***Property size (square footage):*** Generally, larger properties command higher prices. However, flippers should be mindful of potential diminishing returns; exceeding the neighborhood's average square footage might not always translate to a proportional increase in value.

***Number of bedrooms and bathrooms:*** Additional bedrooms and bathrooms are typically viewed favorably by buyers and can significantly increase the value of a property. However, the local market should be considered. In some areas, a four-bedroom house might be more desirable than a five-bedroom one, and strategically converting a smaller bedroom into a well-appointed home office could prove more valuable.

***Condition:*** A property in excellent condition with a well-maintained exterior and a modern interior will likely sell for more than one in need of repairs or outdated finishes. The scope and cost of potential renovations should be factored into the equation to ensure the project remains profitable.

***Upgrades and renovations:*** Strategic upgrades and renovations can significantly enhance the value of a property. Modern kitchens, finished basements, energy-efficient appliances, and features that cater to current lifestyle trends can make a property stand out in the competitive market. However, flippers must be cautious not to over-improve, as recouping the entire cost of high-end renovations might not always be feasible in all neighborhoods.

***Location:*** Properties situated in desirable neighborhoods with easy access to amenities like good schools, parks, shopping centers, or public transportation typically sell for more. Understanding the specific location's influence on value is crucial. A property on a busy street might require a downward adjustment compared to a similar property on a quiet cul-de-sac.

By meticulously evaluating comparable sales and making necessary adjustments, flippers gain a powerful tool for estimating the post-renovation value of a property. This information serves a multitude of purposes. It allows for a feasibility study, determining if the potential profit margin justifies the investment. It empowers flippers to set a realistic asking price, attracting serious buyers while avoiding overpricing the property and leading to a lengthy market stay. Ultimately, the comparable sales approach, when applied with skill and expertise, equips flippers to navigate the market with confidence, making informed decisions that pave the way for a successful property flip. This time-tested technique serves as a compass, guiding investors through the complexities of the market and illuminating the path towards profitable real estate ventures.

***Pros of the Comparable Sales Method:***

In the exhilarating world of property flipping, where calculated risks and informed decisions pave the way for substantial rewards, the comparable sales method reigns supreme as a cornerstone valuation technique. This widely adopted approach empowers real estate investors and flippers to navigate the ever-changing market with confidence, transforming a potentially volatile venture into a lucrative opportunity. Unlike theoretical models or subjective opinions, the comparable sales method boasts a unique advantage: its grounding in undeniable real-world data.

***Unwavering Footing:*** The Strength of Market-Based Valuation.By meticulously analyzing recent sales of similar properties in the surrounding area, flippers gain invaluable insights into current market trends and pricing. These "comparable properties" serve as a benchmark, offering a clear-eyed perspective on the potential value of the subject property after renovations are complete. This reliance on actual sales data translates into a market-based valuation, ensuring the estimated value reflects the true dynamics of the local market. Imagine a flipper considering a property in a neighborhood experiencing a surge in popularity due to the construction of a new school. Traditional valuation methods might not capture this specific factor. However, the comparable sales approach, by meticulously examining recent sales data, would likely reveal a significant increase in selling prices for similar properties in the area, empowering the flipper to capitalize on this valuable market trend.

***Democratizing Knowledge:*** Accessibility for All Levels of Expertise One of the most compelling strengths of the comparable sales method lies in its inherent simplicity and accessibility. The approach itself is straightforward to understand, even for novice flippers embarking on their first project. By focusing on readily identifiable factors like size, condition, features, location, and, most importantly, recent sales prices, the method demystifies the valuation process. This accessibility empowers both seasoned investors and those new to the game to make informed decisions based on clear, objective data. They are not reliant on subjective opinions or guesswork; instead, they have a data-driven foundation for formulating a renovation and pricing strategy.

***Beyond Valuation:*** Negotiation and Pricing Power. The insights gleaned from the comparable sales method extend far beyond simply estimating a property's value. This valuable information equips flippers to strategically position themselves throughout the entire flipping process. By providing a benchmark established by real-world sales data, the comparable sales method empowers flippers to justify their asking price and confidently navigate negotiation discussions with potential buyers. Imagine a scenario where a flipper has meticulously renovated a property, incorporating high-end finishes and desirable features. Comparable sales data from the neighborhood might reveal that similar properties with these upgrades have sold for a premium. Armed with this information, the flipper can confidently enter negotiations, using the data as leverage to secure a sale price that reflects the true value of the renovated property. Furthermore, this data allows flippers to establish a competitive listing price from the outset, attracting serious buyers while avoiding the pitfalls of overpricing and a prolonged market stay. By setting a price that aligns with market expectations, flippers can generate a flurry of interest and potentially spark bidding wars, driving the final sale price even higher.

### Cons of the Comparable Sales Method

***The Data Dilemma:*** Accuracy and Availability. The comparable sales method thrives on a foundation of credible real-world data. However, the accuracy of the valuation hinges on the accessibility and quality of this data. In ideal scenarios, flippers would have a wealth of recent sales data for properties demonstrably similar to the subject property. This includes factors like size, location, condition, features, and amenities. Unfortunately, such a perfect scenario is not always achievable.

Limited data availability can be a significant hurdle, particularly in niche markets or less populated areas. For example, a flipper considering a historic property in a rural location might struggle to find a sufficient pool of recently sold comparables. This scarcity of data can restrict the effectiveness of the method, potentially leading to an inaccurate valuation. Furthermore, the accuracy of the underlying sales data itself is paramount. Errors or inconsistencies in public records can skew the analysis and introduce misleading information into the valuation process. To mitigate this risk, flippers should adopt a multi-pronged approach, consulting a variety of data sources and diligently verifying the accuracy of the information they utilize. Techniques like cross-referencing data points and seeking guidance from experienced appraisers can further enhance the reliability of the data.

***The Ever-Shifting Market:*** Volatility and the Time Factor. The dynamic nature of the real estate market presents another layer of complexity for the comparable sales method. The values derived from comparable sales data represent a snapshot in time, reflecting market conditions at the moment of those sales. However, the real estate market is fluid and constantly evolving. Sudden economic shifts, changes in buyer demographics, or fluctuations in interest rates can significantly impact property values. A valuation based on comparable sales data from several months ago might not accurately reflect the current market climate. Imagine a scenario where a global pandemic triggers a surge in demand for properties with home office spaces. Comparable sales data from pre-pandemic times might significantly underestimate the value of a property that has been strategically renovated to cater to this new market preference.

To address this limitation, flippers should strive to utilize the most recent sales data possible. Ideally, the data should reflect market conditions within the past few months to ensure a more accurate portrayal of current values. In a rapidly changing market, incorporating adjustments to account for anticipated market shifts might also be necessary. Consulting with local real estate professionals or brokers can provide valuable insights into these anticipated market trends, empowering flippers to make informed judgments and adjust their valuations accordingly.

**The Quest for the Perfect Comparable:** The Elusive Ideal. The very notion of "comparable properties" implies a high degree of similarity. In a perfect world, flippers would have access to a selection of recently sold properties that mirror the subject property in every aspect— size, location, condition, features, and amenities. However, perfection is rarely encountered in the real world. Flippers often grapple with the challenge of locating truly comparable properties. Unique architectural styles, highly desirable features, or specific location attributes can make it difficult to find perfect matches. For instance, a property boasting a renovated gourmet kitchen and a sparkling pool might be challenging to compare to similar properties lacking these high-end upgrades. In such cases, flippers must exercise sound judgment and make necessary adjustments to account for the discrepancies between comparable properties and the subject property. This process requires a keen understanding of the local market and the relative value proposition of various features. Does a gourmet kitchen translate to a higher sale price in a particular neighborhood, or would a focus on energy-efficient upgrades be more appealing to potential buyers? Understanding these nuances is crucial for making effective adjustments. Consulting with experienced real estate professionals or appraisers can provide valuable insights into market preferences and help flippers determine the most appropriate adjustments to ensure a realistic valuation.

Let us delve deeper into the practical application of the comparable sales method, a cornerstone technique for property flippers navigating the ever-evolving real estate landscape. Imagine yourself standing at the threshold of a potential flip in a dynamic neighborhood. The property boasts promising features, but before diving headfirst into renovations, you need a clear picture of its after-renovation value. The comparable sales method empowers you to make an informed decision, transforming educated guesses into a data-driven foundation for success.

**1. Define your search radius and criteria:** The groundwork begins with establishing a defined geographic area for your search. Ideally, this should encompass a radius of approximately one mile around your target property. Within this zone, you'll meticulously research recently sold properties that share key characteristics with your subject property. These characteristics form the pillars of your comparison:

**Size:** Focus on houses with comparable square footage. While a precise match might be elusive, aim for properties within a reasonable range (e.g., +/- 10-15% of your target property's size). Do not get hung up on exact square footage; a well-designed layout in a slightly smaller property can sometimes outweigh a larger footprint with an awkward configuration.

**Amenities:** Make a comprehensive list of the amenities your target property boasts— a finished basement, a modern kitchen with high-end appliances, a sparkling swimming pool, or a spacious backyard perfect for entertaining. Prioritize comparables that share a significant number of these amenities. Understanding which features hold the most weight in your target market is crucial for accurate valuation.

**2. Leverage Technology:** Unveiling a Treasure Trove of Data. The Internet has become an indispensable tool for real estate investors. Utilize online databases, property listing websites, and even public tax records to gather information on recently sold properties within your defined area. Many of these resources allow you to filter results based on specific criteria like size, location, number of bedrooms/bathrooms, and even features like pools or fireplaces. Embrace technology to your advantage; the more data points you gather, the more robust your analysis will be.

**3. Analyze and Adjust:** A Balancing Act with Market Nuances. Once you have identified a handful of promising comparables, take a closer look at their selling prices. Here is where your keen eye for detail comes into play. While the sales prices provide a valuable benchmark, you'll likely encounter discrepancies between these comparables and your target property. For instance, imagine you discover a comparable property that sold for $250,000. However, this property boasts an extra bedroom compared to your target property. This difference in size necessitates an adjustment. Knowing the local market, you might determine that an extra bedroom typically translates to a $20,000-$30,000 increase in value. Therefore, you might adjust the comparable's sales price upwards by $25,000 to arrive at a more accurate reflection of your target property's potential value after renovations.

## Beyond the Data: Incorporating a Broad Market View

The comparable sales method offers a powerful data-driven approach, but remember, it is just one facet of a multifaceted evaluation process. Here are some additional factors to consider for a holistic assessment:

*Market Trends:* Is the market in your target neighborhood experiencing an upswing or a downswing? Understanding these broader market forces can influence your valuation adjustments. A hot market might allow you to justify a higher asking price based on anticipated buyer competition, while a cooling market might necessitate a more conservative approach.

***Renovation Costs:*** Factor in the estimated costs of renovations planned for your target property. These costs will ultimately impact your profit margin, so a realistic assessment is crucial. Obtain quotes from reputable contractors to ensure your renovation budget aligns with market rates and avoids unexpected cost overruns.

***Property Condition:*** The overall condition of the property you're considering will influence your renovation costs. A property in pristine condition might require only minor cosmetic updates, while a property in need of significant structural repairs will require a lower initial purchase price to account for the additional investments needed.

***Curb Appeal and Location Nuances:*** Don't underestimate the power of curb appeal and specific location factors. A charming front yard with mature landscaping can significantly enhance a property's value, while a location on a busy street with limited parking might necessitate a downward adjustment.

By combining the insights gleaned from the comparable sales method with a comprehensive understanding of these other factors, you'll be well-equipped to make an informed decision about the potential profitability of a property flip. Remember, the comparable sales method empowers you to approach the market with confidence, transforming calculated risks into the foundation for successful real estate ventures. It's a cornerstone technique

## The Income Approach Method

In the fast-paced world of property flipping, where resourcefulness reigns supreme and calculated risks pave the way for substantial rewards, the income approach method emerges as a powerful tool for valuation. This approach shatters the confines of traditional market value assessments, instead delving into the very essence of a flipper's quest – the income-generating potential of a property. By meticulously analyzing a property's ability to produce a steady stream of rental income, the income approach empowers flippers to make informed decisions that prioritize long-term profitability.

## *A Glimpse into the Future: The Power of Projecting Rental Revenue*

The cornerstone of the income approach lies in its future-oriented perspective. Unlike traditional valuation methods that focus solely on a property's current market value, the income approach compels flippers to envision the potential this property holds. Imagine a scenario where a flipper stumbles upon a property in a developing neighborhood. While the current market value might not be particularly high, the income approach empowers the flipper to see beyond the present. By meticulously analyzing the local rental market, the flipper can estimate the potential rental income this property could generate once strategically renovated and positioned within the rental market. This projected income stream becomes a vital factor when assessing the overall investment appeal of the property. Suddenly, a property that might appear lackluster from a traditional market value perspective transforms into a potentially lucrative opportunity, brimming with the potential for steady rental income over the long term.

## *A Meticulous Journey: Unveiling the Valuation Formula*

The income approach method translates theory into practice through a well-defined roadmap. The journey begins with a **proactive assessment of the local rental market**. Flippers embark on a research quest, meticulously analyzing rental rates for similar properties in the surrounding area. Particular attention is paid to factors that significantly influence rental income, such as the property's size, location, and the amenities it boasts. This in-depth research provides a reliable foundation for estimating the potential rental income the subject property could command after renovations are complete.

With a clear picture of projected rental income, the focus shifts to **calculating the operating expenses** associated with the property. These expenses encompass a variety of ongoing costs that can chip away at a property's profitability. Property taxes, insurance premiums, maintenance fees, and vacancy allowances all fall under this umbrella. A thorough understanding of these expenses is crucial for determining the property's net operating income (NOI), a key metric in the income approach. The NOI represents the actual profit generated by the property after factoring in the operating expenses.

The next step involves unlocking the power of the **capitalization rate (cap rate)**. This metric serves as the bridge between a property's income-generating potential and its estimated value. Traditionally, the cap rate is derived by dividing the property's net operating income (NOI) by its current market value. In essence, the cap rate reflects the expected return on investment (ROI) a property offers. For example, a cap rate of 10% suggests that an investor can expect a 10% annual return on their investment in the property. However, for flippers, the cap rate is typically used in reverse. With the NOI estimated based on projected rental income and operating expenses, the cap rate, obtained from comparable properties or market data, is used to determine the property's value. Imagine a flipper who has meticulously calculated the NOI of a potential investment property to be $20,000 per year. If the prevailing cap rate in the area for similar properties is 8%, the flipper can estimate the property's value based on its income-generating potential to be around $250,000 ($20,000 NOI / 8% cap rate).

Finally, the culmination of the income approach method arrives with the **valuation of the property itself**. By dividing the projected NOI by the cap rate, flippers arrive at an estimated value for the property based on its income-generating potential. This value represents the price an investor would be willing to pay for the property based on the anticipated future rental income stream. It empowers flippers to move beyond a purely market-driven perspective and identify properties that might be undervalued based on current market trends, but hold immense potential for generating a steady stream of income over the long term.

## Pros of using the income approach

***Unveiling the Hidden Potential:*** A Focus on Income Generation. The income approach transcends the limitations of traditional market value assessments. It compels flippers to shift their perspective, focusing on a property's ability to produce income over the long term. Imagine a scenario where a flipper encounters a property in an up-and-coming neighborhood. While the current market value might not be particularly high, the income approach empowers the flipper to see beyond the present. By meticulously analyzing rental trends, the flipper can estimate the potential rental income this property could generate once it is strategically renovated. This projected income stream becomes a vital factor when assessing the overall investment appeal of the property. Suddenly, a property that might appear lackluster from a traditional market value perspective transforms into a potentially lucrative opportunity, brimming with the potential for financial gain through steady rental income over the years.

**Data-Driven Decisions:** The income approach equips flippers with the power of data-driven decision making. By meticulously analyzing projected rental income and operating expenses, flippers can calculate a property's net operating income (NOI). This metric, a cornerstone of the approach, represents the actual profit generated by the property after factoring in ongoing costs. Armed with this information, flippers can estimate the property's value based on its income-generating potential. This empowers them to prioritize properties that offer a strong projected return on investment (ROI), ensuring their flipping endeavors are not just aesthetically pleasing renovations but financially sound ventures with a clear path to profitability.

***Aligning with Market Demand:*** Understanding Rental Market Dynamics. The income approach fosters a strategic alignment with the rental market. By meticulously analyzing rental trends and vacancy rates in the surrounding area, flippers can tailor their renovations to cater to the specific needs and preferences of potential tenants. Imagine a neighborhood experiencing a surge in demand for young professional renters. The income approach empowers flippers to prioritize features that attract this demographic, such as modern kitchens, in-unit laundry facilities, or even co-working spaces. This strategic alignment with market demand not only translates to potentially higher rental income, but also minimizes vacancy periods, ensuring a consistent flow of revenue.

***Beyond the Numbers:*** The income approach, while powerful, should not exist in isolation. Savvy flippers understand the importance of employing this method in conjunction with other valuation techniques to gain a comprehensive understanding of a property's worth. The comparable sales approach, for instance, offers valuable insights into current market trends, while an analysis of renovation costs ensures the projected income stream can realistically cover the investment required to transform the property. When these various valuation methods are used in a complementary fashion, flippers gain a well-rounded perspective, enabling them to make sound investment decisions that account for both the property's income-generating potential and its place within the current market landscape.

***A Tool for Long-Term Strategies:*** The income approach empowers flippers to identify properties with the potential to become long-term cash cows. These are properties that, once strategically renovated and positioned within the rental market, offer the potential for a steady stream of income for years to come. By prioritizing properties with strong projected NOIs and factoring in appreciation potential, flippers can make informed decisions that go beyond the immediate profit generated from a single flip. The income approach empowers them to build a portfolio of income-generating properties, creating a foundation for long-term financial security and sustainable wealth creation in the real estate market.

While the income approach empowers property flippers with a valuable perspective on a property's potential, it's crucial to acknowledge its limitations. Understanding these drawbacks empowers flippers to utilize this approach strategically, mitigating risks and maximizing its effectiveness within their overall valuation strategy.

## Cons of the income approach

***The Crystal Ball Conundrum:*** The Peril of Uncertain Projections. The income approach hinges on the accuracy of two key projections: **rental revenue** and **operating expenses**. Flippers must meticulously research rental trends in the surrounding area to estimate the potential income a property could generate after renovations. However, the future is inherently uncertain. Economic shifts, changes in demographics, or unforeseen events can disrupt rental markets, causing projected income to deviate from reality. Imagine a scenario where a global pandemic disrupts travel patterns and decimates short-term rental income in a tourist destination. The income approach used to assess a property in such a location might have significantly overestimated rental income based on pre-pandemic trends. Similarly, accurately estimating operating expenses can be challenging. Unforeseen repairs, fluctuations in property taxes, or spikes in insurance premiums can lead to unexpected costs, eroding a property's projected profitability. The income approach, while powerful, cannot predict the future with absolute certainty. Savvy flippers should acknowledge this limitation and incorporate a buffer zone when making calculations to account for potential deviations from their projections. Techniques like stress testing, where flippers consider various negative scenarios that might impact rental income or operating expenses, can help them assess the stability of their investment under unforeseen circumstances.

***Beyond Rental Revenue:*** The Neglected Appreciation Factor. The income approach primarily focuses on a property's ability to generate rental income. While crucial, this approach can overlook another significant factor influencing a property's value – **appreciation**. In a healthy real estate market, property values tend to rise over time. The income approach, by solely focusing on rental income, might undervalue properties with strong potential for appreciation. Imagine a scenario where a flipper encounters a property in a rapidly developing neighborhood. The current rental market might not be particularly robust, leading to a lower projected net operating income (NOI). However, the income approach might miss the potential for significant appreciation in the property's value due to the neighborhood's upward trajectory. For flippers who intend to sell the property after renovations rather than holding it as a rental investment, this appreciation factor can be a significant source of profit. Therefore, it's crucial to consider the income approach in conjunction with other valuation techniques, such as the comparable sales method, that account for market trends and potential appreciation. By employing a multi-pronged approach, flippers gain a more comprehensive understanding of a property's value, ensuring they don't neglect the potential for future growth in the property's market value.

*Not a Universal Solution:* The Limitations of Non-Rental Properties. The income approach is best suited for properties intended to generate rental income. However, not all flips fall into this category. Flippers might encounter properties earmarked for owner-occupied living or vacation rentals. In these scenarios, the income approach might not be as relevant. For instance, a flipper considering a property in a desirable vacation destination might prioritize renovations that cater to short-term renters through online rental platforms. While the property might not be suitable for long-term rentals that form the foundation of the income approach's calculations, its value might be significantly influenced by its appeal to vacationers seeking short-term stays. When dealing with properties outside the traditional rental market, flippers should rely more heavily on other valuation techniques like the comparable sales method, which focuses on recent sales data for similar properties, to determine a property's value. Furthermore, consulting with local real estate agents who specialize in non-traditional rental markets can provide valuable insights into factors influencing the value of these unique properties.

## *Example of the Income Approach Method*

Imagine that you estimate this property could generate $1,500 per month in rent after renovations. You have also factored in ongoing expenses like property taxes, insurance, and maintenance, estimating these operational costs to be around $500 per month.

Here is where the income approach comes into play. We'll use a capitalization rate, or cap rate, which reflects the expected return on investment for similar properties in the area. Let's assume a cap rate of 10% for this example. Now, with the estimated income and expenses, we can calculate the property's value based on its potential rental income. We first need to determine the net operating income (NOI). This is calculated by subtracting the operational expenses ($500) from the estimated rental revenue ($1,500), resulting in a monthly NOI of $1,000 ($1,500 - $500). In simpler terms, this is the actual profit the property would generate each month after covering its ongoing costs.

Finally, we can estimate the property's value using the cap rate. We divide the NOI ($1,000 per month) by the cap rate (expressed as a decimal: 0.10). This calculation suggests a property value of $10,000 ($1,000 / 0.10). So, based on the projected income and the assumed cap rate, an investor might be willing to pay up to $10,000 for this property because of its potential to generate a monthly profit of $1,000.

It is very important to remember that the cap rate (10% in this case) is an example, and it can vary depending on the specific market and property type. Researching cap rates for similar properties in the area can provide a more accurate market-driven value.

Do not forget to factor in renovation costs! While the income approach estimates value based on income potential, you'll also need to account for the money spent transforming the property into a rentable state. Subtracting renovation costs from the estimated value will give you a clearer picture of the potential profit from the flip. By understanding the income approach and its limitations, you can make informed decisions when considering property flips, ensuring you factor in both potential income and renovation costs.

## Cost Approach Method:

The cost approach emerges as a cornerstone valuation method. Unlike traditional approaches that rely solely on a property's current market value, the cost approach carves a unique path. It delves deeper, meticulously examining the reconstruction costs associated with the property, empowering flippers to see the potential beneath the surface. Imagine a scenario where a flipper stumbles upon a charming old bungalow in need of some TLC. While the current market value might be underwhelming due to its condition, the cost approach empowers the flipper to see beyond the present. By meticulously analyzing the various cost components, the flipper gains valuable insights that can transform this undervalued property into a profitable venture.

## Building from the ground up: A meticulous reconstruction on paper

The core principle of the cost approach hinges on the concept of **replacement cost**. Flippers essentially embark on a hypothetical reconstruction project, estimating the cost of building a comparable property from scratch on a vacant lot with the same characteristics. This meticulous exercise requires in-depth research into various cost factors:

***Land Value:*** Accurately assessing the value of the land the property sits on is crucial. Consulting with real estate agents or appraisers familiar with the area empowers flippers to unearth the current market value of vacant lots in the surrounding area. Factoring in factors like location, zoning regulations, and potential development trends ensures a comprehensive understanding of the land's worth.

*Construction Costs:* Researching the current costs of building materials, labor, and permits empowers flippers to estimate the expense of constructing a new property with similar features and square footage to the subject property. Resources like construction industry publications, contractor consultations, and online databases provide valuable insights into these ever-fluctuating costs.

## Beyond Reconstruction: Acknowledging the Inevitable Depreciation

The cost approach acknowledges that the property in question isn't a pristine, newly built structure. It incorporates a crucial element – **depreciation**. This refers to the physical deterioration that the existing property has likely undergone over time. Through inspections and consultations with experienced contractors,

Flippers can estimate the cost of repairs and renovations necessary to bring the existing property up to code and make it functionally equivalent to a new build. This depreciation value is then subtracted from the replacement cost, arriving at a more realistic estimate of the property's value that reflects its current condition.

## Pros of the cost approach method

***A Structured Path to Valuation:*** The cost approach offers a systematic and organized framework for property valuation, ensuring flippers don't get swept away in the emotional whirlwind of potential deals. Flippers embark on a well-defined journey, meticulously dissecting the property into its core components – land and building. By meticulously researching the land value in the area and current construction costs, flippers can estimate the replacement cost, which is essentially the expense of building a comparable property from scratch on a vacant lot. This structured approach ensures a clear and well-documented valuation process, minimizing the risk of impulsive decisions based on emotion or incomplete information. Every step is meticulously documented, providing a clear audit trail for the flipper's calculations and a solid foundation for negotiation with sellers or potential lenders.

***A Holistic Perspective:*** Beyond the Purchase Price,the cost approach transcends the limitations of simply considering the property's purchase price. It acknowledges the additional investment required to transform the property to its full potential, empowering flippers to make informed decisions about the total project cost. Flippers factor in the cost of necessary modifications and upgrades, such as renovations, repairs, and replacements. This holistic perspective empowers them to identify properties that might be undervalued based on their current condition but possess the potential to be transformed into valuable assets through strategic renovations. Imagine a scenario where a flipper encounters a property in a desirable neighborhood, but one that requires significant modernization. The cost approach empowers the flipper to see beyond the outdated features and estimate the potential value after renovations are complete. By factoring in the cost of these improvements, the flipper gains a clear understanding of the total investment required and the potential return on investment (ROI). This empowers them to prioritize properties that offer not only a good purchase price but also the potential for cost-effective renovations that maximize their profit margins.

*Valuation for Unique Properties:* The cost approach shines brightest when dealing with unique properties that lack comparable sales data. Imagine a historic property with distinctive architectural features or a custom-built home with one-of-a-kind elements. In such scenarios, the comparable sales approach, which relies on recent sales of similar properties, might not provide an accurate valuation. The cost approach, however, offers a reliable alternative.

By focusing on the underlying costs of land and construction specific to the property, flippers can estimate a fair market value irrespective of the availability of comparable properties in the market. This empowers them to confidently assess the investment potential of unique properties that might otherwise be overlooked. The approach ensures that flippers don't miss out on hidden gems simply because they lack a recent sales history of similar properties.

***Insulation from Market Fluctuations:*** The cost approach offers a strategic advantage, particularly in a dynamic market where trends can change rapidly. Unlike methods that rely solely on comparable sales data, which can be heavily influenced by recent market fluctuations, the cost approach provides a more objective assessment of a property's intrinsic value. It focuses on the underlying costs of land and construction, which are less susceptible to short-term market fluctuations. This empowers flippers to identify properties that might be undervalued based on current market trends, but hold immense potential for value creation through strategic renovations. Imagine a scenario where a flipper encounters a property in an up-and-coming neighborhood. While the current market value might not be particularly high due to the overall condition of the properties in the area, the cost approach empowers the flipper to see the potential for substantial value creation through renovations. By analyzing the land value and construction costs, the flipper can estimate the potential worth of the property after the renovations, making informed investment decisions that capitalize on the neighborhood's upward trajectory. This insulation from market fluctuations allows flippers to focus on the property's long-term potential, making them less susceptible to being swayed by temporary dips in the market.

## Cons of the cost method

**The Mirage of Certainty: The Peril of Unforeseen Costs:** The cost approach hinges on the assumption that flippers can precisely predict the expenses associated with construction and material acquisition. However, the reality of the construction industry can be far more unpredictable. Fluctuations in material costs, unexpected delays due to permitting issues, or unforeseen complications during renovations can significantly deviate from initial cost projections. Imagine a scenario where a flipper encounters issues with asbestos abatement or structural repairs during renovations, leading to substantial cost overruns. The cost approach, based on initial estimates, might have painted a rosier financial picture, potentially leading the flipper to underestimate the total project cost. This highlights the importance of incorporating buffer zones into cost calculations to account for potential deviations and ensure the projected profit margins remain realistic.

**The Blind Spot of Market Forces: A Focus on the Past, Not the Future:** The cost approach primarily focuses on the historical costs of land and construction materials to estimate a property's value. However, the real estate market is a dynamic entity where current and future trends can significantly influence a property's worth. The cost approach, by solely focusing on reconstruction costs, might neglect the impact of factors like market demand, interest rates, and economic conditions. Imagine a scenario where a flipper encounters a property in a declining neighborhood. The cost approach might estimate a high value based on the underlying land and construction costs. However, if the neighborhood is experiencing a downward trajectory, the actual market value of the property might be substantially lower, irrespective of the reconstruction costs. To mitigate this limitation, flippers should use the cost approach in conjunction with other valuation methods, like the comparable sales approach, that incorporate current market trends.

**A Square Peg in a Round Hole: The Challenge of Unique Properties:** The cost approach thrives on standardization. It excels at valuing properties with readily available construction cost data and comparable building materials. However, unique properties with distinctive architectural features or custom-built elements can pose a challenge. Imagine a scenario where a flipper encounters a historic property with intricate woodwork and stained-glass windows. Estimating the cost of replicating these unique features can be complex and expensive, potentially leading to inaccurate valuations through the cost approach. In such cases, the cost approach might underestimate the value of the property due to the difficulty of factoring in the costs associated with restoring or replicating these unique elements. Consulting with specialists in historic preservation or appraisers familiar with unique property types can provide valuable insights in such situations.

## Example Using the Cost Method Approach

Imagine estimating the total cost of buying and meticulously restoring this diamond-in-the-rough to be $200,000. This includes not just repairs and replacements but also strategic upgrades that align with current design trends and neighborhood preferences. Factoring in their knowledge of current market prices for land and building materials, they determined that constructing a brand-new, comparable property on a vacant lot would cost around $180,000. Through the cost approach, they arrive at a preliminary value of $380,000 for the property ($200,000 in renovation costs plus $180,000 in replacement costs).

However, the savvy flipper knows that the cost approach is just the first act in the valuation play. To get a truly accurate picture of the property's worth, they'll likely employ a multi-pronged strategy. One complementary method is the comparable sales approach. This approach involves scouring recent sales data to find properties with similar characteristics—size, location, and features—that have recently sold in the neighborhood. By analyzing these comparable sales, the flipper can get a sense of the market value that buyers are currently willing to pay for similar properties. Imagine if several comparable properties recently sold for an average of $420,000. This data point suggests the market might support a higher valuation than the initial estimate derived from the cost approach.

Another method to consider is the income approach. This approach focuses on the property's potential to generate rental income. By researching rental rates for similar properties in the area, the flipper can estimate the potential monthly or annual income the renovated property could bring in. Factoring in vacancy rates and operating expenses, the flipper can arrive at a capitalization rate, which helps convert that potential income stream into a property value. While the cost approach focuses on the bricks and mortar, the income approach sheds light on the property's potential as an income-generating asset.

By strategically combining these various valuation methods, the flipper gains a well-rounded understanding of the property's worth. They're not just considering the reconstruction costs, but also its market appeal, potential rental income, and overall investment potential. This comprehensive approach empowers them to make informed decisions. Is this property a good fit for their flipping strategy? What's the ideal renovation budget to maximize profit margins? Ultimately, by wielding a multi-method valuation approach, the flipper navigates the exciting world of property flipping with greater foresight, confidence, and the potential to unearth hidden gems that can be transformed into profitable ventures.

## Appraisal Techniques for Flipped Properties

Selling a house—whether it is your permanent home or an investment property—is a huge effort. In any circumstance, you invest a lot of time and money in making the property ready to place on the market, and you need all of that hard work reflected in the assessed value. If you are engaged in real estate investing or if you have been doing a little research before selling your property, you've heard horror stories of appraisal values coming in lower than the seller hoped for. What then?

The finest technique to acquire maximum assessment worth for a property, of course, is to do the work essential to raising the home. Still, it would be helpful to know how to prepare for a home evaluation.

The top three elements to help earn the highest evaluation on your residence are:

***Clean up the yard:*** They say you never have a second chance to establish a first impression, and it's true.

***Obey the $500 rule:*** Spending $500 on some minor fixes may boost your assessment value by thousands.

***Make a list of improvements:*** Appraisers are used to seeing them, and they can check that none of your work is missed.

What Is A Home Appraisal?

A home appraisal, or real estate appraisal, is a professional, objective estimate of the market value of a property. Traditional mortgage lenders need a property appraisal before issuing a loan to safeguard their investment. If a buyer, for example, takes out a mortgage to acquire a property at a price greater than its real market value and subsequently defaults on the loan, the lender may have a hard time selling the property beyond market value to repay their investment.

***Clean Up The Yard:*** An appraiser won't be misled into over-valuing a house based on a wonderful yard, but remarkable curb appeal may start the evaluation on the right foot. Perhaps more critically, the converse is also true: an unkempt yard instantly indicates that the property has not been maintained, and the rest of the assessment will have to work hard to prove that assumption untrue.

Some simple upgrades and considerations may include:

1. Weed flower beds

2. Add fresh mulch to flower gardens

3. Trim up bushes

4. Fill up any bird feeders

5. On the front porch, place one or two potted plants that are young and fresh.

6. Power-wash decks, driveways, and sidewalks (and siding)

7. It could also be good to water the yard and plants more than usual for a few weeks before the inspection. A little added water may make everything seem lush and fresh.

***Obey the $500 Rule:*** There are two sides to the $500 rule.

The first is to take care of those tiny repairs that you may have just grown used to dealing with if you're selling a primary residence. Investing $500 in leaky faucets, malfunctioning light switches, etc. can dramatically improve the evaluation value of the property.

The second aspect of the rule, and the reason why such minor alterations may have such a tremendous impact, is that appraisers tend to work in $500 increments. That suggests that tiny faults will decrease the assessed value, not by the cost of those repairs but by an even $500—every time.

***Make A List Of Upgrades And Repairs:*** If you are new to selling properties, this could seem a touch forward, but appraisers are used to seeing these lists. The list provides many benefits:

1. It alerts the appraiser that you are prepared for their visit.

2. It underlines the labor you've done, so nothing is overlooked.

3. It helps the appraiser appreciate, more generally, how much you have placed in the property.

If you are selling a flipped house, the list might be rather comprehensive, so start with the biggest assets at the top. List each item with the year the repair or upgrade was done. Some upgrades may include something like:

1. Loose floorboard

2. Rain gutters

3. Leaky roof

4. fixed doorbell

5. Dripping pipes or faucets

6. Bathroom caulk

***Research Your Neighborhood:*** There are a few ways that examining your area could aid you in preparing for an examination.

First, you may be able to realize what problems your neighbors had to go through or what unanticipated elements played a role in their assessments. Public documents may show problems that came up during assessments in your neighborhood, but you may also question if you're on good terms with your neighbors.

Second, reviewing recent property prices in your neighborhood can offer you a decent indicator of what to expect for your own.

Finally, developing a second list of neighborhood qualities and amenities could be valuable for the appraiser as well. Location (location, location) is a vital component of any property value. Highlight distinguishing qualities, such as:

1. A new shopping center in the neighborhood

2. Local schools that got an award or have excellent ratings in general

3. Parks, community centers, or trails close

4. Proximity to hospitals or healthcare facilities

5. Newly repaved roads

Make sure you talk about any remarkable aspects of the neighborhood that can add value to your property.

***Host the appraiser:*** Don't go overboard and serve refreshments, but make the appraiser's visit pleasant and uncomplicated. Appraisers are busy and usually make numerous calls in a single day.

Some considerations may include:

1. Set the indoor temperature accordingly. Make sure the dwelling is cool enough in the summer and warm enough in winter.

2. Make sure every space is accessible by pulling in chairs, reducing garbage, cleaning hallways, opening doors, removing baby gates, etc.

3. Crate pets or arrange for them to stay with a friend during the examination. Most appraisers have nightmare experiences involving dogs. Don't let that be your home!

4. Go gentle on fragrances. If you want to use a fragrance or light a candle, remember that everyone has different preferences—and allergies. Use sprays and blow out candles 30 to

60 minutes before the appraiser arrives to make odors inconspicuous.

5. Ensure That Safety Equipment Is Installed And Working.

6. It is easy to forget about safety equipment, especially if the property is your primary dwelling, but appraisers will check. Make sure that smoke and carbon monoxide alarms are installed and batteries are fresh.

7. Home security systems are on and operating well.

8. Fire extinguishers are not expired.

***Clean Again:*** A well-kept property exhibits a well-maintained residence. Cleaning up before the examination might look like a simple effort, but it makes a profound impression on the assessor. All of these things are carefully considered.

Walk around the house with fresh eyes, or ask a genuinely honest friend to come over and help you. Some straightforward steps might include:

1. Removing as much surface clutter as is practicable.

2. Wiping down walls.

3. Shampooing carpets.

4. Cleaning floors to a shine.

5. Bleaching shower grout.

6. Making sure windows are clean and streak-free.

7. Pruning up dark leaves on houseplants.

It may be one day of really rigorous labor, but it could have a big effect on your appraisal worth.

***Look for the small things:*** It is easy to disregard little repairs or improvements—because you have gone blind to them at a permanent residence, or because you've spent so much energy on large modifications on a flip. But too many of those "little things" could have a cumulative, detrimental effect on your assessment score. In addition to the $500 rule, too many little faults date a home (even if you just flipped it). If the perceived age of a property is greater, it will be put into a general group of "older" residences and lose value.

***Rather than waiting till later, have an evaluation done as soon as possible:*** Most appraisals occur when the buyer's lender needs an appraisal as part of the mortgage approval process. If complications come up during that review, however, the sale may just fall through entirely.

Ordering your appraisal when you feel that the home is ready for sale could get you a head start on rectifying any flaws. A typical mortgage lender that gets involved in a possible sale later on will still order their assessment, so the value you obtain from an early appraisal isn't locked in stone. But it may be a fantastic test run, so you can rectify any errors and know what to expect during a buyer's inspection later.

***Invite Your Real Estate Agent Or Realtor:*** A reputable real estate agent will attend the appraisal, particularly if you are unable to go personally, to represent the property. Their knowledge puts them in a great position to discuss similar flip projects or house sales in the same region, as well as local attractions that improve the value of the site. If you are unavailable, the real estate agent may also provide your list of improvements and repairs.

***Do not Crowd The Appraiser:*** This suggestion may seem weird, but not all appraisers prefer having you there all the time. When you follow your appraiser too closely, they sometimes believe you intend to create a diversion or that there is a problem in the house that you do not want them to see. You have to be there to soothe fears and point out highlights, but allow them the freedom to perform their job.

## How To Prepare For An Appraisal

You have already done the work to make considerable repairs and upgrades. You have prioritized high-ROI repairs and upgrades, and done everything you can to greatly raise the value of the property. But you still need to make sure you are conveying the value of the home appropriately, and that happens during the assessment.

Appraisers are specialists, and they have seen a lot of techniques, so you are not going to con them into an unreasonably high evaluation value. But thoroughly preparing for your home evaluation helps ensure that you're transmitting the property's true worth and earning the highest value attainable. Start by wandering about the property with fresh eyes and making a list of modest activities to tackle—small yard work duties, minor repairs, little upgrades, etc.

## Factors Influencing Property Valuation

The world of real estate can be a labyrinth, and property valuation sits at its very heart. Determining a property's worth is no simple feat; it is a captivating blend of art and science, influenced by a complex interplay of factors that go beyond a simple price tag. Let's delve into these key elements that orchestrate the value of a property:

### 1. Location: A Multi-Layer Influence:

The mantra in real estate remains as true as ever: location reigns supreme. However, location's influence extends far beyond mere proximity to amenities like schools, parks, and shopping centers. While these factors undoubtedly play a significant role, a deeper understanding of a property's location unlocks a richer valuation perspective.

***The Neighborhood Tapestry:*** Imagine two identical houses on the same street. One sits directly across from a bustling commercial area, while the other enjoys the tranquility of a cul-de-sac. While both might have easy access to amenities, the one in the peaceful cul-de-sac might command a higher price due to factors like noise levels and privacy. Neighborhood qualities like safety, crime rates, and the overall desirability of the area all contribute to a property's perceived value. A charming bungalow in a quiet, family-friendly neighborhood with a strong sense of community will likely fetch a higher price than an identical property in a high-crime area with transient residents.


***The Allure of Lifestyle and Investment:*** Location also encompasses a property's connection to job centers, transportation hubs, and cultural attractions. A property close to a booming tech hub might attract young professionals, while a location near top-rated schools might be ideal for families. Proximity to airports, train stations, or major highways can enhance a property's value for those seeking convenient travel options. For investors, a property situated in a gentrifying neighborhood with redevelopment plans might hold the potential for significant future value appreciation.

***The Enchantment of Nature's Embrace:*** And let's not forget the allure of scenic vistas! Waterfront views, proximity to natural wonders like mountains or national parks, or landmarks with historical significance can further elevate a property's value, adding a premium for those breathtaking backdrops or a connection to a rich heritage. Imagine a charming cottage nestled amidst rolling hills with a panoramic view of a lake compared to one in a crowded urban setting. The tranquility and beauty of the natural surroundings can significantly influence a property's value proposition.

## 2. Unveiling the Heart of the Home: Beyond Square Footage:

Beyond the facade lies the heart of the home—its size, layout, and functionality. The number of bedrooms, bathrooms, and living spaces significantly influences a property's value. A spacious home with a well-designed, open floor plan that fosters a sense of flow and connection will generally be more valuable than a cramped one with awkward room configurations that feel disconnected and isolating. However, square footage alone doesn't tell the whole story.

***Functional Design for Modern Living:*** Modern buyers prioritize functionality and efficient use of space. Smart storage solutions, built-in features that maximize space utilization, and flexible living areas that can adapt to different needs can significantly enhance a property's value. Imagine a home with a cleverly designed mudroom that provides ample storage for shoes, coats, and backpacks, reducing clutter in the main living areas. This type of functional design appeals to busy families seeking organized and efficient living spaces.

***The Allure of Unique Charm and Modern Amenities:*** The property's condition also plays a vital role. A well-maintained home with a recent history of repairs and upgrades using high-quality materials will naturally garner a higher price compared to one in disrepair. Unique features and amenities can also set a property apart from the competition. A sparkling pool, a cozy fireplace, a chef's kitchen with high-end appliances, or a finished basement that can be converted into a home theater or recreation room can add a touch of luxury and elevate the property's value proposition for discerning buyers.

### 3. The Market's Pulse: A Symphony of Economic Forces:

The ever-shifting tides of the market significantly impact property valuations. Supply and demand dynamics play a critical role. If there's a surplus of houses on the market with few buyers (high inventory, low buyer activity), property values might stagnate or even dip. Conversely, a seller's market with high buyer competition and low inventory can drive prices upward. Understanding these dynamics empowers sellers to time the market strategically and investors to identify potential buying opportunities.

## 4. Unveiling the Power of Cash Flow: Income Potential:

For investors venturing into the realm of rental properties, the property's income-generating prowess takes center stage. Here's how income machinations influence valuation:

***Dissecting Rental Income Streams:*** A keen analysis of the property's potential to churn out rental income is paramount. This meticulous process involves researching rental rates for similar properties in the area to estimate the gross rental income – the total annual rent collected before accounting for expenses. Operating expenses, such as property taxes, insurance, maintenance costs, and vacancy rates, are then factored in to arrive at the net operating income (NOI), the lifeblood of any rental property, representing the actual cash flow generated by the property. A property with a strong potential for positive NOI becomes a highly sought-after investment opportunity, attracting investors seeking a steady stream of income.

***Valuation through the Lens of Income Capitalization:*** Investors also employ sophisticated metrics like capitalization rates (cap rates) and gross rent multipliers (GRMs) to estimate a property's value based on its anticipated income stream. The cap rate acts as a shorthand ratio, expressed as a percentage, that relates the NOI to the property's current market value. A lower cap rate generally indicates a more stable and desirable investment with a higher potential return on investment. Similarly, the GRM offers a quick valuation tool. It's the ratio between the property's value and its gross rental income. A high GRM might suggest the property is undervalued, while a low GRM might indicate it's overpriced relative to its income potential. By wielding these metrics, investors can make informed choices, prioritizing properties that marry strong rental income potential with a favorable risk-reward profile.

## 5. The Cost of Replacement: A Balancing Act Between Age and Potential

The cost approach to valuation, previously explored, revolves around the concept of replacement cost—the estimated expense of meticulously rebuilding the property from the ground up on a vacant lot using current construction costs and materials. While replacement cost offers a valuable benchmark, it's crucial to consider two additional factors to arrive at a more comprehensive valuation:

***The Inevitable March of Depreciation:*** As a property ages, it succumbs to the relentless march of wear and tear. Functional utility might diminish due to evolving design trends or technological advancements. These factors contribute to depreciation, which acts as a hidden thief, steadily stealing away from the property's value over time. The cost approach doesn't automatically account for depreciation. A shrewd appraiser will factor in the property's age, condition, and any signs of functional obsolescence to arrive at a more realistic valuation that reflects the property's current state and marketability.

***Location's Enduring Allure: Value Beyond Bricks and Mortar:*** Imagine a historic property nestled in a prime location. While the replacement cost might be lower due to the use of older building materials and techniques, the property's value might be significantly higher due to its location, historical significance, and unique architectural features. In such cases, the cost approach might underestimate the property's worth, highlighting the importance of considering the property's specific characteristics and market appeal. A well-preserved historic property in a trendy neighborhood might attract a premium from buyers seeking a piece of history with modern conveniences, even if the underlying building materials are not the latest and greatest. Location injects a timeless value proposition that can transcend the limitations of the cost approach.

***6. Legal and Regulatory Landscapes: Understanding the Rules of the Game***

The legal and regulatory environment surrounding a property can significantly impact its value and development potential. Here's how these factors influence the valuation equation:

***Zoning and Development Constraints: A Roadmap for Potential.*** Zoning Regulations dictate the game of property use – residential, commercial, industrial, or agricultural. These restrictions can limit the potential uses for a property and consequently affect its value. For example, a property zoned for single-family homes might be less valuable than an identical property zoned for multi-unit dwellings in a market with high rental demand. Similarly, land use constraints, such as easements or setbacks, might restrict development options or limit the size and type of structures that can be built on the property. A savvy investor will always research zoning regulations and development limitations before finalizing a purchase, ensuring the property aligns with their investment plans and can be developed according to their vision.

## 7. The Allure of Trends and the Power of Perception: A Dynamic Duo Shaping Value

Consumer preferences are like the ever-shifting sands on a beach, constantly evolving and shaping the landscape of what's deemed desirable in a property. Here's how these trends, coupled with market perception, influence value:

***The Ever-Evolving Landscape of Consumer Preferences:*** Imagine two side-by-side townhomes built in different eras. One features a maze of compartmentalized rooms, catering to a bygone era of formal entertainment. The other boasts an open-concept floor plan with seamlessly integrated living spaces, perfect for modern lifestyles that prioritize connection and flow. The open-concept design, catering to a desire for functionality and a sense of togetherness, will likely command a higher price in today's market. Keeping abreast of these trends empowers sellers to stage their properties strategically, highlighting features most coveted by modern buyers for investors, understanding these preferences allows them to identify properties with in-demand features and the potential to appreciate as those trends gain traction. However, market perception adds another layer of complexity. A vintage property in a historic district might be perceived as having more character and charm than a newly built home, even if it lacks the modern amenities of the latter. A savvy appraiser will consider both the tangible aspects of a property, like its layout and features, and the intangible allure associated with its location, architectural style, and potential for customization.

**The Mystique of Location: Beyond Tangible Amenities.** A property's value is not solely defined by its physical location. The market's perception of a location's reputation, historical significance, and overall vibe plays a significant role. A charming cottage nestled in a historic district with a vibrant arts scene and a reputation for walkability might hold a premium for those seeking a unique lifestyle experience, even if it lacks the sprawling lawns and large lots found in newly developed suburbs. A savvy appraiser will consider both the tangible aspects of location, like proximity to schools and parks, and the intangible allure of a neighborhood's reputation and character. This perception can be further amplified by a community's commitment to sustainability, its investment in green spaces and local businesses, or its proximity to cultural attractions and entertainment hubs. All these factors contribute to a neighborhood's unique cachet, influencing how desirable – and valuable a property within that location becomes.

## 8. The Broader Canvas: External Factors Shaping the Market Symphony

The world of real estate doesn't exist in a vacuum. Macroeconomic trends, geopolitical events, and global economic circumstances can all exert a powerful influence on the property market, acting as a conductor in a complex symphony of value:

***The Pulse of the Global Economy:*** Investors with a keen eye on the bigger picture understand how broader economic trends impact real estate markets. A strong global economy with low interest rates might fuel investor confidence, leading to increased demand for properties and potentially driving prices upwards. Conversely, an economic downturn or rising interest rates can dampen investor sentiment and lead to market stagnation or even price corrections. By understanding these macroeconomic forces, investors can make informed decisions about when to enter or exit the market and navigate the inevitable cycles of boom and bust. This knowledge also empowers them to identify undervalued properties in distressed markets with the potential for significant appreciation when economic conditions improve.

***Embracing Technological Advancements: Shaping the Future of Property Value.*** The world of technology is constantly evolving, and the real estate market is not immune. Properties equipped with smart home features like automated lighting systems, voice-controlled thermostats, or security cameras can command a premium from tech-savvy buyers seeking convenience and a connected living experience. Similarly, properties located near public transportation hubs slated for upgrades or in areas with planned infrastructure advancements like high-speed rail lines might see their value appreciated due to the promise of improved accessibility and connectivity. Investors who stay abreast of these technological advancements can identify properties poised to benefit from these innovations and capitalize on their future potential. Furthermore, advancements in sustainable building practices and renewable energy technologies can also influence property values. Eco-conscious buyers might be willing to pay a premium for properties with energy-efficient features, such as solar panels or rainwater harvesting systems, as these elements translate to lower operating costs and a reduced environmental footprint.

# Managing Financial Aspects: Mortgage Loans and Total Cost of Ownership

In order to effectively manage the financial elements of real estate, it is necessary to evaluate the overall cost of ownership and have a solid grasp of mortgage loans "Let's delve deeper into each of these factors to understand their impact on property value."

### *1. Home Loans: Mortgages*

A mortgage loan is a specific kind of loan that is meant to be used for the purpose of financing the acquisition of real estate. It makes it possible for people or organizations to get a loan from a lender (such as a bank or mortgage company) in order to acquire a property, with the property itself acting as collateral for the loan.

Mortgage loans come in a wide variety of forms, including fixed-rate mortgages, adjustable-rate mortgages (ARMs), government-insured loans (such as FHA loans and VA loans), and specialized loans for specific purposes (such as jumbo loans for high-value properties or construction loans for building new homes).

There are several mortgage loan options available to choose from. The terms of a mortgage loan normally include the loan amount, the interest rate, the repayment schedule, and any additional restrictions that may be applicable. The terms of the loan may change based on a number of circumstances, including the creditworthiness of the borrower, the amount of the down payment, and the conditions that are currently present in the market.

*Process:* In order to acquire a mortgage loan, applicants are often required to submit an application to a lender and supply many pieces of documentation, including proof of their income, job history, credit reports, and information about their assets. The lender assesses the borrower's financial background and property facts to establish eligibility and loan conditions.

***Repayment:*** Borrowers repay the mortgage loan over time, generally via monthly payments that include both principle (the amount borrowed) and interest (the cost of borrowing). The repayment schedule might vary based on the kind of loan and parameters agreed upon between the borrower and lender.

***Consequences:*** Mortgage loans have substantial financial consequences for borrowers, including the amount of money borrowed, the interest rate applied to the loan, and the overall cost of borrowing throughout the life of the loan. Borrowers should thoroughly assess their financial status and capacity to repay the loan before taking on mortgage debt.

## 2. Total Cost of Ownership:

***Definition:*** The total cost of ownership (TCO) refers to the entire expenditures involved with owning and maintaining a property over a certain period of time, beyond the original purchase price. It covers numerous expenditures, including mortgage payments, property taxes, insurance, upkeep, repairs, utilities, and homeowner association (HOA) fees.

***Components:*** The TCO of a property encompasses both one-time expenditures (such as closing charges and upfront fees) and continuing costs (such as recurrent expenses and periodic maintenance). Understanding these components helps buyers and homeowners budget and prepare for the whole cost of homeownership.

***Calculation:*** To calculate the TCO of a property, buyers and homeowners should consider all relevant expenses associated with owning and maintaining the property, including mortgage payments, property taxes, insurance premiums, maintenance costs, utilities, and any other fees or expenses specific to the property or location.

***Budgeting:*** Budgeting for the TCO of a property lets purchasers and homeowners analyze affordability, prioritize costs, and prepare for future financial commitments. It helps guarantee that they can easily pay the connected expenses of housing without exceeding their financial capabilities.

***Planning:*** Planning for the TCO of a property entails reviewing anticipated expenses, forecasting future costs, and maintaining a cash reserve for unforeseen or emergency expenditures. It helps purchasers and homeowners anticipate and handle financial difficulties proactively, decreasing the chance of financial distress or foreclosure.

# Exploring Mortgage Options for Financing Flips

Exploring mortgage possibilities for funding flips means analyzing numerous loan choices designed for real estate investors who seek to acquire, repair, and sell houses for profit. Here's additional information about these mortgage options:

## 1. Fix-and-Flip Loans:

*Purpose:* Designed primarily for real estate investors who want to acquire homes, remodel them, and sell them rapidly for a profit.

*Features:* Fix-and-flip loans often provide short loan periods, ranging from six months to two years, to coincide with the timeframe of the refurbishment and selling process.

*Requirements:* Lenders may ask for a down payment of 20% to 30% or more, depending on the borrower's creditworthiness and the property's condition.

*Interest Rate:* Interest rates for fix-and-flip loans are frequently higher than standard mortgage rates owing to the short-term nature of the loans and the increased risk involved with real estate investing.

*Approval Process:* Approval for fix-and-flip loans is focused primarily on the property's prospective worth following rehabilitation rather than the borrower's credit score or income.

## 2. Hard Money Loans:

*Purpose:* Hard money loans are short-term loans offered by private investors or lending businesses, commonly employed by real estate investors for rapid funding without the necessary paperwork needed for regular loans.

*Features:* Hard money loans often feature higher interest rates and costs compared to standard mortgage loans but provide speedier approval and financing, making them suited for time-sensitive transactions.

***Requirements:*** Hard money lenders concentrate more on the property's worth and prospective profitability than the borrower's credit history or income.

***periods:*** Hard money loans normally have shorter periods, ranging from six months to a few years, and may include balloon payments or interest-only installments.

### 3. Lines of credit or loans secured by the home's equity:

***Purpose:*** Home equity loans or lines of credit (HELOCs) enable homeowners to borrow against the equity in their main property to fund real estate transactions, including fix-and-flip projects.

***Features:*** Home equity loans and HELOCs often provide lower interest rates compared to fix-and-flip loans or hard money loans but necessitate utilizing the homeowner's principal house as collateral.

***Requirements:*** Borrowers must have sufficient equity in their house to qualify for a home equity loan, or HELOC, and lenders may put restrictions on the amount they may borrow depending on the property's assessed value and the borrower's creditworthiness.

***Longer periods:*** Home equity loans and HELOCs frequently offer longer payback periods compared to fix-and-flip loans, giving borrowers greater flexibility in managing their cash flow.

**4. Private money loans:**

***Purpose:*** Private money loans entail borrowing from people or private investors, frequently via personal relationships or networking within the real estate business.

***Features:*** Private money loans provide flexibility in terms of loan terms, interest rates, and repayment schedules since they are arranged directly between the borrower and lender.

***Requirements:*** Private money lenders may be more flexible in their lending requirements compared to conventional lenders, but applicants still need to show the capacity to repay the loan and provide a credible investment proposal.

***Relationship-Based:*** Private money loans depend on personal ties and trust between the borrower and lender, making them suited for experienced investors with established networks.

### 5. *Crowdfunding or peer-to-peer lending:*

***Purpose:*** Crowdfunding platforms and peer-to-peer financing networks link real estate investors with individual investors who give cash for fix-and-flip projects.

***Features:*** Crowdfunding and peer-to-peer lending allow access to financing from various investors, sometimes with cheaper interest rates and fees compared to conventional loans or hard money loans.

***Requirements:*** Investors must submit their fix-and-flip project on the crowdfunding platform or peer-to-peer financing network and fulfill specific requirements to qualify for funding, such as showing the property's potential profitability and giving comprehensive project plans.

***Online Platforms:*** Crowdfunding platforms and peer-to-peer lending networks exist online, enabling quick access to funds for real estate investors and chances for individual investors to diversify their investment portfolios.

## Calculating Total Cost of Ownership

When purchasing new equipment, the price tag only gives you half of the picture. Energy expenditures, maintenance, and repair fees are typically many times greater than the original price! But frequently, they are left unconsidered and contain deadly surprises later down the road. Calculating the Total Cost of Ownership is a critical stage when planning new investments. What is the total cost of Ownership (TCO)?

There is an adage amongst sailors concerning sailboats that says: "The only good times are when you buy it and when you sell it.". This tends to suggest that the ownership itself is nice but may have some negatives too. Calculating all the expenses a new purchase may tag along includes not just the original price but also its operation, maintenance, downtime, output, and lifespan - all of these play into the total cost of ownership and are always dependent on the exact purchase made.

## The relevance of the total cost of ownership

The essential thought is that every time there is a buy, you need to evaluate more than the expenditures or the investment at the moment of the transaction. Ownership and use of a given piece of equipment, a product, or a service have a cost too. These charges could vary substantially throughout the solutions that are given.

When examining alternatives when it comes to making a purchasing option, customers should look not merely at an item's short-term price, the so-called purchase price. But customers should also look at its long-term price, or rather, its total cost of ownership (TCO). The item with the lowest total cost of ownership has the greatest value in the long term.

## How is the total cost of ownership calculated?

Originally, the phrase TCO was taken into account when firms and individuals were seeking to acquire assets or make investments in capital projects. The ultimate purchase choice was based on the calculation of adding Capital Expenditures (CAPEX) to a large purchase that would be utilized in the future with Operating Expenditures (OPEX), which reflect day-to-day use costs.

### *Total cost of ownership and the supply chain*

In the world of supply chain management, there is a hidden truth lurking behind the initial purchase price. While it might seem like the most important factor, focusing solely on that number can lead to misleading conclusions. This is where the total cost of ownership (TCO) comes into play. TCO takes a more holistic approach, factoring in all the expenses incurred throughout the entire supply chain. This includes everything from acquiring raw materials and manufacturing the product to warehousing, transportation, and finally getting it delivered to your customer. By taking a broad look at these additional costs like storage, logistics, and potential quality issues, TCO reveals a surprising fact: the initial purchase price often represents a surprisingly small portion of the overall financial picture.

This deeper understanding empowers supply chain managers to make informed decisions that go beyond the initial price tag. For example, a supplier offering a seemingly lower upfront cost might not be the most economical choice in the long run. Unreliable delivery schedules can disrupt production, and frequent quality problems can lead to returns and rework, both of which add hidden costs. By factoring these elements into the equation, TCO analysis helps identify these hidden expenses and allows companies to choose suppliers who optimize efficiency and minimize overall costs across the entire supply chain.

## Managing Cash Flow and Expenses Effectively

Managing your cash flow is one of the most crucial things required for your company to flourish, especially when operating in a capital-intensive sector such as real estate.

Managing and improving cash flow is vital for the financial performance of your real estate firm, the absence of which may hamper development, limit investment prospects, and generate financial stress. To avoid this scenario from recurring, here are effective tactics that may help you control the influx and outflow of cash in your real estate firm.

***Expand Service Offerings:*** You may enhance your company's revenue inflow by extending your service offerings beyond typical property sales. This may include property management services, real estate advice, or related services such as interior design or staging.

By diversifying your services, you may establish extra sources of regular income that will help stabilize cash flow throughout the year.

***Develop Referral Networks:*** Another strategy to enhance revenue inflow is by developing strong referral networks with similar industry specialists, such as mortgage brokers, house inspectors, or contractors, which may lead to a regular flow of recommendations.

By cultivating these connections and offering outstanding service, you may get referral fees when their suggested customers complete purchases.

***Focus on Long-Term Client Connections:*** Building long-term client connections is crucial to creating recurring revenue. Encourage customer loyalty by delivering great service, keeping frequent contact, and giving value-added services such as market updates or educational materials. Repeat customers create steady commission revenue and represent a key source of recommendations, adding to a more reliable cash flow.

***Cutting Operating costs:*** This may be performed by identifying and cutting needless costs, which is vital for maximizing cash flow.
You should examine your agency's expenditures and seek out areas where costs may be cut without sacrificing the quality of service, such as negotiating advantageous terms with suppliers, investigating cost-effective marketing methods, and establishing efficient operating procedures. Controlling expenditures may free up funds for investment and development prospects.

***Implementing Effective Receivables***

***Management:*** Timely collection of receivables is vital for maintaining a constant cash flow situation. You must develop clear payment conditions and rules to be shared with your customers and follow up carefully on delayed payments.

Consider introducing automated invoicing systems and software such as Xero and Quickbooks, which provide handy payment choices to facilitate quick payments. Effective receivables management can help eliminate cash flow gaps and enhance the overall financial health of your organization.

***Building Cash Reserves:*** Maintaining a cash reserve is critical for handling unforeseen costs, market volatility, and seasonal swings in real estate activity. You should adopt a systematic strategy for creating cash reserves by putting away a percentage of your agency's revenue. Having cash reserves promotes stability, minimizes dependency on loans, and prepares your agency to capture new possibilities in the market.

# Navigating Market Dynamics: AvoidingManipulation

Understanding market dynamics and avoiding manipulation is vital for each investment. Following are some crucial methods to consider: Understanding Red Flags:

*Unusual Volume:* Sudden spikes or drops in trading volume with minor price changes might suggest manipulation. For instance, a stock price could climb considerably with heavy volume, but if that volume originates from a single major investor, it might be an effort to create a misleading sense of demand.

*Unrealistic News:* Be careful of unexpected, unsubstantiated favorable news articles around a specific investment. These might be created to increase pricing. Cross-reference news with trustworthy sources and follow the company's real performance.

***Pump-and-Dump Schemes:*** These schemes include artificially increasing the price of an asset by generating favorable buzz (typically on social media) and then swiftly selling after unwary investors join in, leaving them with a deflated investment. Be careful of unsolicited investing advice online.

Research and Due Diligence:

***Dig Deeper Than Headlines:*** Don't base judgments only on news items or social media trends. Research the company's financials, analyze its previous performance, and grasp its industry prospects.

***Focus on Fundamentals:*** Look for organizations with excellent fundamentals, such as continuous revenue growth, profitability, and a quality management team. These variables are less vulnerable to alteration.

***Verify Information:*** Double-check information from press releases or corporate announcements with official filings and reports from independent financial organizations.

## 1. Develop a disciplined approach

***Stick to Your Investment Plan:*** Do not change your long-term approach based on short-term market volatility or emotional reactions to news.

***Diversify Your Portfolio:*** Spread your assets across multiple asset classes and businesses to lessen risk. This helps limit the effect of manipulation in any particular market.

***Invest for the Long Term:*** A long-term investing perspective helps you to weather market volatility and lessens the temptation to make hasty judgments based on manipulative methods.

## 2. Staying Informed

***Follow Reputable Sources:*** Rely on recognized financial news channels, research companies, and independent analysts for investing information.

***Learn About Market Manipulation:*** Educate yourself on typical manipulation strategies so you can detect them and avoid falling victim.

***Be Skeptical of Unrealistic Claims:*** If something appears too good to be true, it generally is. Don't go after unrealistic returns or get caught up in frenetic shopping sprees.

By adopting these tactics, you may become a more knowledgeable and careful investor, more prepared to negotiate market dynamics and avoid the traps of manipulation. Remember, there's no alternative to extensive study, a disciplined approach, and remaining informed.

## Recognizing Market Manipulation Tactics

Market manipulation is a critical topic in the realm of third market creation since it may dramatically damage the fairness and integrity of financial markets. Detecting and preventing market manipulation involves various hurdles for regulators, market players, and technology vendors alike. In this part, we will look into some of the primary challenges encountered in this quest and discuss alternative solutions to solve them. One of the key obstacles to identifying market manipulation lies in the intricacy and sophistication of the strategies deployed by manipulators. These people or organizations frequently use different loopholes or engage in deceptive methods to artificially affect market prices, create misleading trends, or fool other market players. Identifying such manipulation needs modern data analysis techniques and algorithms that can spot aberrant patterns or irregular trade actions.

The fight against manipulators is an endless loop as they constantly refine their techniques, forcing regulators and technology vendors to perpetually adapt their strategies.

Another problem derives from the huge volume of data that has to be evaluated to discover possible instances of market manipulation. With the introduction of high-frequency trading and the spread of computerized trading platforms, the volume, velocity, and diversity of data have increased. Analyzing this vast volume of data in real-time to identify tampering becomes a demanding undertaking. Furthermore, differentiating between genuine trading methods and manipulative operations may be tricky since many trading patterns may look identical on the surface but have distinct underlying motives.

Lack of transparency in some markets adds to the difficulty of identifying and combating market manipulation. In certain situations, manipulative behaviors may occur in dark pools or over-the-counter marketplaces, where trading activity is not publicly revealed. This opacity makes it tougher for authorities to monitor and uncover deceptive conduct. The ever-evolving challenge of market manipulation lies not only in the continuous adaptation of manipulators' techniques but also in the inherent complexities of the markets themselves. Exploiting cross-market inefficiencies and engaging in coordinated trading across diverse platforms make it incredibly difficult to pinpoint the source of manipulation. This is why effective mitigation hinges on a collaborative effort – regulators, market participants, and technology vendors must work together to outmaneuver these sophisticated schemes. Unite and fight manipulation! Sharing knowledge, best practices, and real-world cases (case studies) strengthens our collective defense and hones our ability to spot these tricks. For example, the Financial Industry Regulatory Authority (FINRA) in the United States runs a Market Manipulation Unit that aggressively investigates and prosecutes manipulative behavior. By using their experience and sharing information with market participants, they add to the industry's overall capacity to identify and avoid manipulation.

Technology plays a significant role in tackling the difficulties of market manipulation. Advanced surveillance systems integrated with machine learning algorithms may help spot suspicious patterns or actions that may suggest manipulation. These algorithms can evaluate huge volumes of data, including trading data, news feeds, social media sentiment, and even alternative data sources, to identify possible manipulation. By continually improving these tools and adding new data sources, market players and regulators can keep ahead of manipulators and lessen the danger of market manipulation.

Case studies and instances of successful detection and prevention of market manipulation are useful in learning the techniques adopted by manipulators and devising effective responses. For instance, the "Flash Crash" of 2010, when the Dow Jones Industrial Average had a sudden and dramatic collapse, led to regulatory reforms and improvements in market monitoring systems. By examining such incidents and learning from prior failures, market players and regulators may strengthen their capacity to recognize and avoid manipulation.

## The Elusive Target: Regulatory Challenges in Unmasking Market Manipulation

Market manipulation is a misleading activity that compromises the integrity of financial markets, distorts prices, and erodes investor trust. As such, regulators play a critical role in identifying and combating market manipulation to maintain fair and transparent trading conditions. However, this work is not without its problems. From technical improvements to developing market dynamics, authorities confront various difficulties in their attempts to efficiently detect and counteract market manipulation.

**1. The hallmark of market manipulation lies in its deceptive nature:** Manipulators utilize sophisticated strategies that are often difficult to uncover. These strategies vary from conveying misleading information to establishing fake demand or supply, all aimed at manipulating pricing for personal advantage. Identifying these deceptive activities requires authorities to be aware of the newest strategies deployed by wrongdoers.

For example, "spoofing" is a strategy where traders place big orders with no intention of executing them, attempting to create a false appearance of market activity. Detecting spoofing requires authorities to evaluate enormous volumes of trade data and trends to identify real orders from manipulative ones.

**2. *Rapid Technological Advancements:*** The emergence of high-frequency trading (HFT) and algorithmic trading has considerably enhanced the pace and complexity of market transactions. While these technologies have provided efficiency to markets, they have also introduced new potential for market manipulation.

HFT algorithms may conduct transactions within microseconds, making it tough for authorities to keep pace with manipulative behavior. Additionally, manipulators may exploit loopholes in algorithmic trading systems or employ sophisticated tactics like "quote stuffing" (flooding the market with a huge number of orders) to disrupt regular market functioning.

**3. *Cross-Jurisdictional Challenges:*** In today's linked global marketplaces, market manipulation frequently crosses national lines. Regulators encounter problems in coordinating activities across countries owing to disparities in legislative frameworks, regulatory standards, and enforcement capacities.

For instance, a manipulator working from one nation might target stocks listed in another jurisdiction, making it tough for authorities to adequately investigate and punish such crimes. Cooperation and information exchange between regulatory agencies have become vital to successfully preventing cross-border market manipulation.

**4. *Limited Resources:*** Regulators typically confront resource limits, including financial limitations and personnel challenges. The sheer amount of trading activity and the intricacy of market manipulation tactics require enormous resources to monitor and investigate possible incidents.

With limited resources, authorities may struggle to devote sufficient manpower and technology to adequately identify and prevent market manipulation. This constraint may hamper their capacity to

## *Outsmart the Market: 10 Strategies for Savvy Investors*

House flipping, although potentially profitable, involves inherent hazards. However, by adopting a set of well-defined tactics, you may considerably boost your chances of success and preserve your investment throughout the process. Here is a summary of major areas to concentrate on, along with extra considerations to reinforce your risk-mitigation strategy:

## Pre-Purchase Due Diligence:

***Market Analysis:*** Conduct rigorous market research. Target communities with growing property prices, great demographics (good schools, low crime rates), and indications of ongoing renovations, which might signify a future hot market,. Don't only depend on internet materials. Talk to local realtors, contractors, and investors to gain a well-rounded view of the market dynamics and possible hidden gems.

***Property Selection:*** Focus on homes with "good bones." Prioritize a sturdy foundation, a fair layout, and a lack of serious structural difficulties. Cosmetic upgrades are often less costly and time-consuming than structural repairs. Consider hiring a trained inspector to do a complete review of the property's condition and find any possible faults before you purchase.

***The 70% Rule:*** Utilize this rule to avoid overspending. Ideally, your offer shouldn't exceed 70% of the After Repair value (ARV) minus the expected repair expenses. This creates a cushion for unanticipated costs and maintains your profit margin. Don't be hesitant to haggle the purchase price, particularly if the house needs considerable modifications.

Strategic Renovations:

***High-Impact Upgrades:*** Prioritize improvements that give the most substantial return on investment (ROI). Kitchens, baths, and flooring often have the largest effect. However, carefully examine the overall functioning of the room. An additional bedroom or a completed basement might considerably improve the property's value, depending on the location and buyer demographics.

***Cost-Effective Approach:*** Avoid splurging on premium finishes. Opt for contemporary, neutral modifications that appeal to a wide spectrum of purchasers and optimize your ROI. Focus on creating a clean, bright, and attractive area that helps prospective buyers visualize themselves living there.

***Curb Appeal Enhancement:*** First impressions are essential. Invest in landscaping, a new coat of paint, and cleaning up the doorway to boost the property's visual appeal and attract prospective buyers. Consider adding things like a well-maintained mailbox or an inviting porch to make a pleasant first impression.

## *Financial Management:*

***Finance Options:*** Secure the correct financing depending on your project demands. Factor in remodeling expenditures, holding costs (mortgage, taxes, insurance), and unforeseen expenses. Consider hard money loans, but be wary of possibly higher interest rates. Explore other financing choices, including private lenders or fix-and-flip mortgages, but ensure you understand the terms and circumstances properly.

***Building a Trusted Team:*** Assemble a team of seasoned experts. This should include a trusted contractor for improvements, a realtor specializing in selling flipped residences, and a financial adviser to aid with budgeting and cash flow management. When assessing contractors, acquire references and verify their licenses and insurance. Don't be scared to acquire many offers before making a selection.

## Exit Strategy Considerations:

***Market Timing:*** While the future is unclear, avoid flipping during home market downturns when selling could be difficult. Consider market trends and economic projections while determining your project schedule. Stay updated about local market circumstances and be prepared to change your departure plan if required.

***Budget for Contingencies:*** Always include a cushion in your budget for unanticipated repairs or permit complications. Unexpected expenses might derail your profit margin if not accounted for. Factor in extra expenditures like garbage collection, permits, and temporary lodging during repairs.

***Competitive Pricing and Staging:*** Work with your agent to price the home competitively in the current market. Additionally, stage the property to reveal its full potential and attract purchasers immediately. High-quality images and virtual tours may also be essential in enticing prospective purchasers in today's digital era.

***Additional Safeguarding Measures:***

***Limited Liability Company (LLC):*** Consider incorporating an LLC to build a barrier between your personal assets and any liabilities emerging from litigation or accidents during repairs. This might help you secure your own cash in the event of unanticipated occurrences.

***Comprehensive Insurance:*** Obtain comprehensive property insurance and general liability insurance to protect yourself from any dangers linked with the refurbishment and ownership stages of the project. General liability insurance may protect you from financial damages if someone is harmed while visiting the property during renovations or open houses.

***comprehensive Budget and schedule:*** Create a comprehensive budget for improvements and a realistic schedule for project completion. This can help you remain on track financially and minimize cost overruns or delays that might harm your profit margin. Regularly assess your progress and budget, and be prepared to alter your goals if required.

## *Staying Informed About Market Trends and Regulations*

Real estate investing, the monolithic arena where fortunes are formed and aspirations are moored, is as much an adventure of the intellect as it is a trip of the heart. As a real estate investor, your success rests primarily on your ability to foresee market trends with clarity and insight. But in an ever-shifting global economy, how can one expect to remain afloat and plan a route to a safe harbor?

**Cultivating Market Intelligence:**

***Curated News Sources:*** Develop a tailored list of respected financial news sources and industry-specific publications. Regularly watch these sources for insights into market movements, economic statistics, and developing trends that might effect your company's choices. Consider The Wall Street Journal, Reuters, or Bloomberg for wider market news, with specialist periodicals pertinent to your particular sector.

***In-Depth Market Analysis:*** Seek out research papers and analysis from established financial institutions, investment banks, and research businesses. These papers give significant, in-depth insights on market trends, industry outlooks, and prospective investment possibilities that closely correspond with your area.

***Industry Engagement:*** Actively engage in industry organizations and attend their conferences, seminars, and webinars. These events offer a venue for industry experts to discuss vital insights about market trends, possible disruptions, and best practices for managing a changing world.

Regulatory Monitoring:

***Government Resources:*** Bookmark the websites of important government agencies and regulatory authorities. These sites are the official source for information on new legislation, compliance requirements, and forthcoming changes that might have a direct influence on your company's operations.

***Legal Expertise:*** Partner with a knowledgeable legal practitioner specializing in your sector. They may give specialized counsel on navigating complicated regulatory settings, ensuring your organization stays compliant, and avoiding the legal risks associated with non-compliance.

***Industry Alerts:*** Subscribe to industry-specific newsletters and alerts that keep you updated about regulatory changes and legal developments influencing your field. These customized updates guarantee you don't miss vital information that might damage your operations.

*Leveraging Technology:*
***Market Data Platforms:*** Explore online platforms that provide market data, real-time updates, and complex analytics tools. These tools may aid you in recognizing trends, analyzing competitor activity, and making

data-driven choices that are strategically aligned with current market dynamics.

***Compliance Software Solutions:*** Consider deploying software solutions intended to ease regulatory compliance for your firm. These solutions may automate activities, monitor crucial dates, and provide thorough reporting, helping you stay up-to-date with the newest rules and reduce the risk of non-compliance.
Maintaining Vigilance:

***Dedicated Information Gathering:*** Establish a regular pattern for reviewing news sources, government websites, and industry magazines for updates. Allocate particular time slots in your plan for information gathering to ensure you stay current on market trends and regulatory changes.

***Professional Networking:*** Connect and create ties with other professionals in your sector. Attending business networking events and cultivating open contact with colleagues may be a beneficial method to exchange information and ideas while simultaneously remaining updated about market trends and prospective regulatory changes.

# Conclusion: Your Journey to Success in House Flipping

In conclusion, going on a trip into the world of home flipping may be both thrilling and rewarding. Throughout this course, we've addressed the foundations of flipping properties, from understanding market dynamics to navigating financial elements and mitigating risks. By equipping yourself with information and taking proactive actions to educate yourself, do due diligence, and keep watchful, you're more suited to succeed in this business.

Remember, success in home flipping involves patience, effort, and a willingness to adapt to changing market circumstances. As you navigate through the ups and downs of the real estate market, believe in your instincts, draw on the experience of trusted advisers, and stay dedicated to your investment objectives.

Whether you are a seasoned investor or just starting out, the route to success in home flipping is a continual learning process. Embrace adversities as chances for progress, enjoy your wins, and learn from your failures along the way. Above all, keep your eyes on the ultimate goal: to create value, produce profits, and establish a profitable real estate portfolio. With effort, persistence, and a smart approach, your route to success in home flipping is within grasp. So, go ahead with confidence, and may your activities in the realm of real estate bring you riches and satisfaction.

## Recap of Key Concepts and Strategies

Let's summarize the important principles and tactics discussed in this guide on home flipping:

***1. Understanding House Flipping:*** House flipping entails acquiring houses at a reduced price, remodeling them, and selling them for a profit. It's a sort of real estate investment that needs careful strategy, execution, and market understanding.

**2. Investing goals:** Before going into home flipping, it's vital to determine your investing goals. Consider aspects such as expected returns, risk tolerance, and investing timetables to develop clear objectives.

**3. Market Dynamics:** Understand the local real estate market, including trends, supply and demand dynamics, and price patterns. Stay updated about market circumstances to make smart investing choices.

**4. Financing possibilities:** Explore several financing possibilities for house flipping, such as fix-and-flip loans, hard money loans, home equity loans, or private money loans. Evaluate the terms, conditions, and fees of each choice to determine the best match for your needs.

**5. Due Diligence:** Conduct rigorous due diligence before acquiring a property. Research the property's condition, market worth, comparable sales, and remodeling expenses to determine its investment possibilities appropriately.

**6. Risk Management:** Mitigate risks connected with home flipping by diversifying your portfolio, being watchful for warning indicators, and avoiding speculative activity or market manipulation.

**7. Remodeling Strategies:** Develop a remodeling plan that adds value to the property while maintaining budget and timetable limits. Focus on high-impact enhancements that attract consumers and optimize returns on investment.

**8. Selling techniques:** Implement efficient marketing and selling techniques to attract prospective buyers and achieve the intended sale price. Consider staging the home, utilizing internet platforms, and working with professional real estate agents to speed the selling process.

*9. Financial Management:* Manage funds properly throughout the home flipping process by analyzing spending, creating a contingency reserve for unanticipated charges, and optimizing cash flow to optimize earnings.

*10. Continuous Learning:* House flipping is a dynamic and ever-evolving profession. Stay current on market trends, regulatory changes, and best practices via continual education, networking with industry leaders, and learning from both triumphs and mistakes.

## Encouragement to Take Action and Pursue Your Real Estate Goals

Now that you've received insights into the world of home flipping and equipped yourself with vital information and methods, it's time to take action and pursue your real estate objectives with confidence and drive. House flipping provides a route to financial freedom, wealth building, and personal satisfaction. By grasping chances, accepting difficulties, and exploiting your gained experience, you may begin on a fulfilling road towards success in the real estate market.

Do not allow fear or uncertainty to hold you back. Instead, put your energy and drive into real activities that move you closer to your objectives. Whether you're a seasoned investor or a newbie enthusiast, there's no better time than now to enter the thrilling arena of home flipping. Remember, every great investment began with a single step. So, dare to dream large, establish bold objectives, and commit to making them a reality. Embrace the process, learn from your experiences, and adapt to the ever-changing environment of real estate. As you negotiate the highs and lows of the home flipping adventure, be tough, keep focused, and stay inspired. Surround yourself with like-minded folks, seek help from mentors, and celebrate your victories along the way.

Above all, trust in your ability, believe in your vision, and never underestimate the power of persistence. With effort, tenacity, and a positive outlook, you have the ability to achieve incredible success in the world of real estate. So, go ahead, take that initial step, and begin on your road to real estate glory. Your future awaits, and the possibilities are boundless. Dare to follow your dreams, and watch as they blossom before your eyes.

## Resources for Further Learning and Support

As you continue your adventure into the world of home flipping and real estate investing, it's crucial to have access to great resources for additional learning and assistance. Here are some suggested sites to deepen your knowledge and boost your skills:

1. Bolster your house flipping strategy with expert advice. Consider picking up some of the acclaimed books on the subject. They offer valuable guidance on everything from market

analysis and property selection to renovation budgeting and effective sales techniques.

2. Online Courses and Webinars:
*Udemy:* Explore courses in real estate investing, home flipping, renovation ideas, and financial management.
*Coursera:* Enroll in courses given by universities and industry professionals covering many elements of real estate investing and home flipping.
*BiggerPockets:* Access webinars, tutorials, and instructional resources on real estate investment, home flipping, and property management.

3. Podcasts:
*BiggerPockets Podcast:* Listen to conversations with successful real estate investors, home flippers, and industry professionals, providing insights, ideas, and techniques.
*The Real Estate Guys Radio Show:* Tune in to talk about real estate investing techniques, market trends, and wealth-building ideas.

***The Ultimate Real Estate Investing Podcast:*** Gain expertise from conversations with elite real estate investors, entrepreneurs, and thought leaders in the business.

4. Online Communities and Forums: ***BiggerPockets:*** Join an online community of real estate investors, home flippers, and industry experts to ask questions, share experiences, and network with like-minded people.

***Reddit's Real Estate Investing Community:*** Engage with other investors, exchange ideas, and engage in conversations about real estate investing strategies, market trends, and best practices.

***Facebook Groups:*** Join relevant Facebook groups focusing on real estate investing, home flipping, and property rehabilitation to interact with peers and receive useful information and assistance.

5. Local real estate associations and meetings:

a. Attend local real estate investing clubs, meetings, and networking events in your region to connect with seasoned investors, hear from guest speakers, and exchange ideas with other enthusiasts.
b. Join local chapters of real estate groups such as the National Association of Real Estate Investors (NAREI) or Real Estate Investment Association (REIA) to access educational courses, seminars, and networking opportunities.

6. Mentoring Programs and Coaching:

Consider obtaining mentoring or coaching from experienced real estate investors or house flippers who can give specialized direction, advice, and support targeted to your individual objectives and issues.

By accessing these resources for extra study and assistance, you may continue to develop your knowledge, polish your abilities, and negotiate the complexity of the real estate market with confidence and success. Remember to be interested, keep involved, and never stop learning as you pursue your real estate ambitions.